LIFE

WHAT I LEARNED ABOUT AMERICAN LIFE WHILE HUGGING MY AMERICAN WIFE

Decio de Carvalho

Faithful Life Publishers
North Fort Myers, FL
FaithfulLifePublishers.com

Life

Copyright © 2011 Decio de Carvalho

ISBN: 978-1-937129-12-5

Published, printed, and distributed by:
Faithful Life Publishers
3335 Galaxy Way
North Fort Myers, FL   33903

www.FaithfulLifePublishers.com

info@FLPublishers.com

Scripture quotations from the King James Version.

Printed in the United States of America

19 18 17 16 15 14 13 12 11   1 2 3 4 5

DEDICATION

This book is dedicated to a little American boy whose birth alone has demonstrated to the world that every human life has divinely-determined worth, meaning, and purpose. His name is Trig Palin. A toddler at this writing, Trig has, from birth, been given the honor of being a national, living symbol of the dignity of human life. He inherited this honor through the bravery of his wise mother who defied the ominous secularization of our culture. She did this at a time when America desperately needs to remember that there is a Creator Who fashions human beings *"in His Own image and likeness"* for purposes which *"eyes have not seen, nor ears heard, neither have entered into the heart of man"*; a Creator Who graciously shares with us this pleasurable responsibility. She did it with her own body and at the risk of her popularity and her future as a national leader.

In the year 2040, may a handsome Mr. Trig Palin and brave Mom be still with us, still signaling to our nation the worth of every human life, whether already among us or still in the womb. May mother and child Palin still be demonstrating then how tragically wrong secular humanists are in stealing from God His divine prerogative of determining who among us should live and who should die. May history have proven by that time that it is naturalism that is a myth, not God, the Creator of the Universe. May scientists and philosophers such as Princeton's Professor of Ethics Peter Singer, who pontificates that,

> "By 2040 it may be that only a rump of hard-core know-nothing religious fundamentalists will defend the view that every human life, from conception to death, is sacrosanct... [T]he fact that a being is a

human being, in the sense of a member of the species homo sapiens, is not relevant to the wrongness of killing it."

be proven to be false, soulless prophets, and may the Pilgrims' America still be a Nation Under the God of Creation.

I want to dedicate this book also to minorities of Americans of every color and background whose only sure hope of equality rests on America staying as founded -- under God Who created the whole of humanity in His image and likeness -- not on the latest political ideology decrying a Creator God.

As an American By Choice, I want to dedicate this book also to all God-fearing, family-loving immigrants to America who, like me, fell in love with this nation for what she truly is, not just for what she so generously gives. It was for such a country that we gave up all the little or much that we had, to become Americans. We understand that today, those who want to recreate the America of our desire into a nation of their own imagination want our votes to accomplish such a purpose. May we, late-coming Pilgrims to America, discover, before it is too late, what truly caused America to be the unique nation that she is; how her singular identity is being marred and threatened with unwanted, needless change. May we discern that we might have been brought here "for such time as this", and that this, too, like every human birth, was for the right purpose. Like the Jewess Esther, may the Pilgrims' Judeo/Christian God help us to frustrate the heretical plans of secularists.

D. de C.

APPRECIATION

It is not every writer who has the privilege of having his manuscript edited professionally by a Ph.D. who enjoys writing, reading, teaching in a Seminary, and editing what other writers write. This scribe did, not only in having his scribbles' shortcomings detected and pointed out, but also for having David Ford, Ph.D. as a close friend. A famous writer of the past said that a good writer is the one who knows which words should be left in the inkwell. This humble Professor helped me condense hundreds of single-spaced typed pages into the current 160 page book. My gratitude is beyond the richest words and needs not his editing; because it is from the heart, a simple "Thank you, David!" will have to do.

But I have a confession to make. After my friend returned the edited manuscript to me I made quite a few changes and additions on my own and refrained myself from burdening David with further editing. For penalty, I have to admit being sole responsible for any English infraction the reader finds in the book. What grammarians call "barbarism" is not easy to avoid when you write in a learned language as I did. I find English preposition—as cradle-Americans' vernacular appropriately says—real "killers".

And what am I to say about Olivia, my dear wife, this tower of spiritual strength, faith, and wisdom hidden in gentle femininity whom my Creator blessed me to have as my life's companion? Needless to say, as the title of this book indicates, without Olivia the whole work would have remained in the inkwell.

Our good friends, Tony and Melissa Paglieri, together with my son-in-law, Robert Williams, teamed up to guide this old typist through the mysteries of a computer's word processing system. Thank you, Tony and Melissa! Thank you, Robert!

Then, there are the people that coordinated the printing of my book - Faithful Life Publishers. Both Jim Wendorf, Founder and Una, his wife, when contacted, promptly made themselves ready and willing to personalize their publishing skills to meet my needs. And their approval of this book's message was a source of much encouragement to me. Thank you, Jim and Una.

D. de C.

ONE

SPIRITUAL ALZHEIMER'S?

"Bless the Lord, O my soul, and forget not all his benefits:
... who redeemeth thy life from destruction." (The Psalms)

Unlike the other patients, the man just wheeled into the meeting-room didn't seem old or weak enough to need the wheelchair. Until you saw his eyes. Life seemed to have already vacated them. They stared at you out of their emptiness. You felt helpless and dispirited while looking at him, realizing that all you could do was look and keep silent. His fingers were fumbling with a lever by the chair's armrest as if on their own volition. Their movements didn't denote any visible purpose. You would think that somewhere in the depths of the man's dying brain there was a feeble message being issued in connection with a lever which operated... a brake? A door back to freedom, to light, to life? But to the middle-aged man the difficulty of the task was obviously insurmountable. His fingers' response was not being transmitted back to his enfeebled mind, and the groping continued, repetitious, fruitless. This motion was the only indication that life had not entirely departed from the strong body being wheeled about by somebody else's will and energy. His face remained a constant blank throughout our visit.

Even after the music.

"That's Captain Andy," the Activity Director informed us. "He's only 50. Until recently, Andy was flying Boeing 747's."

We had played our music and sung our songs to the group of Alzheimer patients whom the staff had guided or wheeled into the meeting-room. As usual, the response from most of them was gratifying. The mellow sounds of the harp had quieted down the mumblers and calmed the fidgety ones. The Mozartean music, with its harmonious, balmy sounds, had brought quietness and expectancy into the crowded room. The traditional hymns lovingly brought back from the past by my wife's magic fingers at the piano had moved a few of them to happy tears and pleasant smiles. Some even joined us in singing, faces now aglow with the recollection, pleased with themselves for their accomplishment of the moment.

But the music had done nothing for Captain Andy. He was still sitting there, lethargic, expressionless. His plodding fingers were still caressing the wheelchair lever - a throttle? - like a blind man reading Braille. Could it be that in his state of mind, the world where his short-circuited brain landed him was filled only with dials, gauges, computers, the sophisticated devices his fingers so dexterously commanded just a short time ago - just before weakened or misdirected pulses misconnected in his body, taking away from him a world so real to sentient human beings but now only a darkness to him? Would he clear his murky runway in time to avoid an impending imagined crash?

Andy seemed not to have a chord of life left within him to be awakened by an outside musical touch. Wasn't there any memory of light formed and cherished in his past which could break the darkness that comes at life's end? Wasn't there any trace of vivifying information left somewhere inside of him, something tuned to respond to sounds that still vibrated in his ears or to the outside light still filling his eyes? How can expiring lives which love once conceived no longer respond to love? While watching Andy suffer silently, my heart ached with the thought that though still physically there, he himself, as a soul, was not. A steel wall separated him from us and from everything else.

Later, harp and stools loaded back in our old RV, Olivia and I sat down to evaluate the program. I needed to think further about the reason why I had the image of our Nation in the back of my mind while looking at the wan faces before us. It all started while watching Andy's pathetic attempt to operate the lever on his wheelchair. An interpreter within me had captioned the word "America" under the emotive picture. Now trying to rest, I sought to discover the logical, credible link connecting in my mind our Nation to the mentally debilitated airline pilot and his companions in dementia.

The silent suggestion was that there was a parallel between the sad state of our Country today and the depressing scene of mental illness we had been witnessing. Is a nation what their people are, or what they think they are? Can she become what people become? Is a nation's soul a composite of her children's souls? Balking at the portent of the analogy, I resorted to praying. As I prayed for Andy in his fading life, I found myself praying for America in the same breath. For she is no longer the same Country which I thought of as a healthy, virtuous nation when I chose her as my home over fifty years ago.

It was while praying that I saw the full, heartbreaking picture: America is doing things contrary to the character she inherited from those who conceived her because she no longer knows who she truly is. She has lost, somehow, a sense of reality. Her illness started when she turned her back on the God of her fathers as Creator, the God Whom her Founders acknowledged and honored. She no longer remembers how often she was warned by those who conceived her of the horrible consequences she should expect for backsliding as a nation. She is no longer believing as factual the Biblical account of the origin of life which gives human beings their incalculable worth. She is forgetting the truths that lead citizens and nations to truly reliable resources to meet life's needs. She no longer knows that our Nation's Fathers had, wisely, impregnated the new Nation with a true, vital knowledge about human life which enabled her to birth and adopt children with the means to secure what is required to live meaningfully - children properly equipped to meet new circumstances and needs being developed in the course of time and history. She is forgetting that faith is what generated the healthy birth of America, her Fathers having been seeking justice from the time of her conception; that America can only live by that faith or languish without it, for as the Holy Scriptures teaches, *"the just shall live by faith"*.

Like Alzheimer's patients, America doesn't seem conscious of what she is doing. Like Andy, too many Americans can no longer remember, or they only remember vaguely and wrongly. I was seeing in Andy the new generation of a unique Nation's children who have never found out, have forgotten, or have been lied to about America's true identity - people who don't know what the Founders of their nation knew, heartily believed, and wisely applied to her foundation, principles that were capable of making it strong enough to support her desired greatness.

As I mourned for Andy that evening, I found myself mourning for America, both of them no longer being their noble selves. I mourned for the new generation of Americans not aware of the sterling beginning and values which enriched the singular nation of their birth. I mourned for a Country that sacrificed the lives of a multitude of her children in foreign wars to bring humaneness to lands enslaved by tyranny, today "making eyes" with those whose God-denying socio-political beliefs have brought hellish suffering and death to millions. I mourned for those Americans who paid the ultimate price for our freedom, their suffering parents and children now seeing that freedom being dissipated in the present atmosphere that affirms political systems and values foreign to America.

I mourned for the millions of would-be Americans murdered in the womb by the choice of once humane lovers - baby souls put to flight in the throes of pain before they could happily identify themselves as Americans; human beings dying before becoming, by God's ongoing creative designs, what millions of people all over our suffering world would gladly be. I mourned for the deluded surgeon who used his skilful hands to snuff out the life of the person to whom our Creator could have intended to reveal how to cure Alzheimer's disease, as He has been doing through American physicians regarding other illnesses through the years. I mourned for a Land that once chose to sacrifice the lives of half a million of her children to die in a Civil War that she might live up to her Godly belief in human freedom, worth, and dignity, now allowing millions more to perish so as to keep hedonism alive. I mourned for a nation whose human warmth was once powerful enough to thaw out a Cold War and bring down its rude wall, now enamored with the same Godless political philosophy of its cruel builders. All of this, all of this because America no longer knows who she is; because of the loss of the true meaning and worth of human life created by God for purposes so great as to be beyond matter and time - the values that made up her true identity.

Since that day, the words I need in praying for America often fail me.

I find myself weeping instead.

TWO

DEMENTIA OR DECEPTION?

"I have set before you life and death, blessing and cursing; therefore choose life, that both thou and thy seed may live." (Moses)

Historians and politicians have been arguing ever fiercely in our cultural courtroom about what has made our nation prosperous and mighty, and what defines her identity. Today in America, now past being a duo centenarian, the jury is still in session - needlessly, with their votes seemingly equally divided. Throughout the long contestation - again, needless - the arguing turned into a Cultural War which continued to get uglier even while America's spiritual health declined visibly. Has America developed dementia after years of exercising the sound judgments she inherited from her Fathers, or had her enemies within and without her who contested her true identity succeeded in deceiving her? If the latter is the case, has she reached the point where she can never be her gentle self again, again wisely ministering to the human needs of her children and of the world through her might and good-heartedness?

Before falling asleep that emotive evening when meeting Andy, I entreated my feelings to give my mind more room for reasoning. The fair nation I fell in love with in my youth now a victim of dementia? For half a century I had been studying the reasons for America's greatness as a nation. I had been noting her sins along with the virtues which once surpassed her faults. I had been chronicling in my mind through the years the gradual changes in her socio-political behavior which so saddened me. But I never foresaw in her a mental illness in the making. America, a victim of spiritual Alzheimer's? That could never happen to so healthy a nation, I thought. Could this suggestion of dementia be a ploy used by the Archenemy of life, the Master Deceiver of humanity, to delude me also? Was he trying to disturb my thinking by having Captain Andy's piteously groping fingers pluck the strings of this immigrant's tender heart? Emotionally and physically tired, I fell asleep before I could answer these questions.

For years I have felt that if my observations concerning the visible moral decline of the nation which I and the world so admired were to be published as a book, "beguilement" would have to be the active word in explaining her change of behavior, not "Alzheimer's". No cure for this illness has been found yet, but deceit is a contrived disease, an inducement to unbelief, not a form of fatal dementia. It can be cured. In this case, the picture wasn't, and isn't, so hopeless. Eventually I became convinced that it was indeed through deception that Americans, citizens of the most successful nation in human history, have been made to ignore what had caused their nation to be what she has become. And deception can be successfully treated with sound reasoning, faith, and prayer. That conclusion sparked in me the hope of yet seeing America recovered.

This hope bore with it some pertinent questions. What could make American children remember or discover their Nation's unique identity which "The First Comers", as the Quakers called the Pilgrims, envisioned when grafting in her their very souls? Can a pristine understanding of what our Founders had in their minds when conceiving and founding this Nation be duplicated in the minds and hearts of a post-modern citizenry? How are the people to realize that there were more inspirational reasons besides the fantasized American "streets of gold" attracting people from all over the world to come here and make America their home? Can Americans still be made to prize the distinctive contents of her Declaration of Independence, the Birth Certificate which so clearly reveals her true identity through her openly acknowledging a God of Creation? Can they realize that our unique Constitution is not a mere booster used to carry America to heights of accomplishments and then to be discarded as obsolete equipment? That instead, it was intelligently designed to serve as a perennial launching vehicle furnished with all that is needed for whatever time and circumstances require for further and farther travels? What medicine can be given or what can be said to Americans to make them discover or rediscover the America whose attributes made up the light of Winthrop's and Reagan's *"City on a Hill"*? Does a "late-comer" Pilgrim like myself, who chose America for what she really is - or was - not just for what she can, and still so generously gives, have a role in helping our Nation find her true self again? Is there anything that can be done to keep her from ending up an ignoble Country, her glory remembered only by others than herself, as Andy's stature is now remembered only by his caring nurses and never by his companions in dementia? If nothing can be done to restore America to her right senses, will our Nation be taken over by a soulless horde of sophisticated skeptics and atheists in the same way rich, but decadent Rome was conquered by the barbaric inhumanity of heathens?

It took some time before I was to find answers to these questions. But find I did. The picture is now clear to me: too many Americans have been indeed deceived. The deception is fueled by a wrong interpretation of human life, something contrary to what America's Founders believed, and contrary to the identifying features of the nation they created. They acknowledged the truths about life's origin that impart to it meaning, worth, and purpose, and planted a nation upon them. Together, the truths about the origin of human life and about the birth of America are what gave this unique Nation her true identity and birthed her greatness. Man-made theories about both beginnings have been artfully, assiduously taught to two or three generations of Americans. These deceptive untruths are the forces that have been gradually weakening America and dragging her to the brink of self-destruction where she stands today. This makes America's present problem of identity one of a spiritual nature.

I am not a preacher or a prophet, and I don't want to sound like one in attempting to articulate successfully the truths held by the Founders of the Nation I love and have chosen as home. But you don't have to be either to do it. When not tampered with by self-serving revisionists, America's history is a textbook on the nature of God and Man. It is a historical fact that our Nation was conceived and reared in a faith in the God of the Judeo/Christian Holy Scriptures. This fact is at the very core of the exceptionalism that makes America a nation as unique in history as the Jewish nation whose people refused to die even after two millennia of dispersion - a nation which the Pilgrims sought to emulate when conceiving America.

I am not a statesman, either, who happens to be a believer, to explain how spirituality fits into the field of polity; how our believing Founders and equally God-fearing leaders who followed them succeeded in keeping the two separate yet working together; how their coexistence was prolonged enough to assure our nation's growth into greatness; how those leaders managed to keep our nation from the obvious danger of sliding into the same theocratic-like, tyrannous elitism that forced those who conceived America to seek refuge in the New World. I thought that by telling my story, though being just another run-of-the-mill member of her society's rank and file, I could assist my betters to retrieve life's true meaning from the trash bin where naturalism is disposing it. Today, as never before in human history, the picture of life as created by God - and not just spontaneously sprouted out of slime - must be exhibited in the marketplace of our Nation. The secularization of America by a God-denying Academia backed by a proud, dishonest Science, a complying educational system, and a biased communication industry must be made to cease if the health of our society is to be restored.

This book is my small contribution to accomplish this purpose. I realize now that the title I have chosen for it perhaps is too candid for the taste of most Americans. But my enormous debt of gratitude to America can only be paid with the legal tender of honesty. I had to settle for it since it refers to the actual experience when I was made fully aware of the most important, yet perilously ignored, truths about human life and how crucial they are for America today. It was while actually hugging Olivia, my cradle-American wife now of over fifty years, that I finally saw life as our Creator sees the life He created. Through the years, Olivia faithfully mirrored to me the America I always thought America was like since hearing about this unique nation in my childhood. Though vulnerable to the same deceptive ruses of education and culture, Olivia never changed as America did. She still exhibits today the original attributes and ethos of the Founders' America which I got to know so well. The reader will learn more about my revealing hugging experience later on.

My only credential for writing this book is that, like the proverbial chicken, I stumbled across a diamond while pecking for life's meaning in a yard littered with human ideas. But unlike the chicken who walked away disappointed because the jewel was not a grain of corn, I took my discovery to heart, soul, and body. I was elated in being fortunate enough to realize the true meaning, purpose and worth of the gem called life. Because of this experience, my own life is richer today. Life in America can still be richer too, if she will only return to her Fathers' God as the God Who created life with all the meaningfulness and joy this truth brings.

I know today the very source of my adopted Country's ills and how she can be cured. I am ready now to write a book about it. The worth of the jewel I have found is high enough and its meaning plentiful enough to be displayed, shared, and still have it for myself, whole. That's how rich human life is. I can't help but cackle happily about my finding.

That's what inspired the book you have in your hands.

THREE

PROGRESS OR INSANITY?

"Saul, Saul, why persecutest thou me?...it is hard for thee to kick against the pricks." (The Creator of life)

To the world at large of today, and to both cradle-Americans and Americans By Choice old enough to have lived here at a time when there was a healthy measure of socio-political soundness, insanity seems like the word to describe what has been recently happening to America. It is difficult not to diagnose as irrational a civilized nation that calls a same-sex union a marriage and the misguided duo a family and still prides herself on being rational. And how can sophisticated members of this Nation's Supreme Tribunal acknowledge themselves to be incapable of defining pornography unless their minds are twisted? How can they quibble the exact time a baby developing in the womb is to be considered a human being in order to decree whether its killing is a crime or not unless their judgment is impaired? How can our judges and politicians call our Constitution, the proven rock-solid foundation of the most successful nation in human history, a "living thing", thus subject to the vagaries of time and history to which it must surrender the floor and scepter, unless their thinking is distorted? Or to hold that to have all the money in the world being equally divided among its people would make us all rich, not paupers still?

But the ultimate symptom of folly which seems now an integral part of our culture is the willful ignoring of the proven mathematical impossibility of the spontaneous genesis of human life. Despite all our sophistication, we allow ourselves to insist on believing that two plus two equals five, not four, and think of it as true science, not cheating. Or, worse, we fail to see this guess-work as an indication of self-inflicting dementia. Isn't the voice of history as loud and as clear as it can possibly be when asserting to the world how naturalism with its cheapening of human life was what facilitated the killing of millions in the last few years? Haven't we learned anything from the madness of Stalin, Hitler or Mao? How can sane, intelligent people fail to perceive this naturalistic definition of life as the hidden procurer of the lethal weapon of meaninglessness behind the grim statistics of fratricides, suicides, and infanticides? Was Malcolm Muggeridge too rash when writing that our present culture has been *"educated into imbecility?"*

If human life as defined by naturalists is just what you see looking back at you from the coldness of a mirror, blossomed into being only to wither and become, in time, mingled forever with matter-teeming earth; if the body you see in it happens to be a malformed shell in which you live, with no hope of compensation or redress for as long as your vital organs work properly; if the tender baby you rock in your arms today is only a temporarily fresh model of the wasted body to be carted away tomorrow, never to be seen again; if our deep longing for what is good and enduring is but the fancy of neutrons pulsating in our short-lived brain cells only to fade forever into nothingness someday; if all the beauty we see and sense can suddenly disappear from our view at any time, never again to delight our souls; if eyes blind at birth must be closed in death without ever seeing the loveliness of a flower garden or a golden sunset, their enchantment having never warmed their hearts; if the deaf-mute and the unloved are condemned to never feel the warm sound of "I love you" for no fault of their own; if those pulses electrically induced in your brain supposedly by nature alone are the only explanation we have for that poem within you begging to be written, or that landscape pleading to be painted; if only conditioned reflexes are behind a savage's beastly destructiveness of human life and a cultured man's rational killings of fellow human beings; if there is not an endless source of unfailing hope for every wrong and every imperfection in our world and in our lives to be made right some day; if there is no assurance that injustices shall be done away with, that wrongs shall be righted and only good prevail, with relativism no longer blurring the difference; if these perceptions of life are all we can glean from our culture to provide us with what we need to fill our hearts with a satisfying measure of joy and peace and enrich our lives with meaning - then our teachers about life are willing accomplices in yet unredeemed Nature's cruelest of all practical jokes. They are the modern version of pharisaical iconoclasts bent on destroying our divinely inherited, sacred desires for purity in meaning.

If life is what atheistic science tells us it is, then human beings are left deprived of truly worthy values and poor in virtuousness, condemned to act like the beasts whom Darwinists purport to be our siblings. Only nervous sensations with the insatiability of glandular pleasures are left to be entrusted with the impossible role of gratifying our yearning for the deeper, purer pleasures that compose the soul-food of joy. Children are robbed of their childhood through the raping of their innocence; the vanishing of their wholesome aspirations resulting from our culture's deformed "realism" and the bareness of its existentialism. Hastened into a dissatisfying adulthood, they shall reach it only to see themselves as life-long prey to disenchantment. No one should be surprised, then, when teenagers decide on their own which day should be their last.

Reason, acclaimed in our present culture as the lauded attribute of the false god-man of science, should applaud when the lives of millions of innocent babies considered disqualified as human beings are snuffed out in throbbing pain before their delicate facial muscles can learn to smile and, in due time, to laugh. Yet, she can only cringe before such barbarous scenes. She hides her face in horror and shame against the whiteness of Hippocrates' toga when a well-educated physician purposely causes the old and the ill to die because their undefined "quality of life" has dwindled down to memories - when their contribution to a secularized society no longer meets a guessed requirement. And if another unfulfilled sharp-shooter deliberately exterminates the lives of those around him with a blast of bullets before ending his own, all that secular academic elitists can do is try to ignore the tragedy and look the other way in the vain hope that evolution will eventually overcome evil. Blind or insensible to the blood on their hands, they shall continue to lecture those still living on the "myth" of a Creator of splendors; they shall go on leading our society away from the Author of the ultimate, immutable pattern by which to distinguish good from bad, right from wrong, truth from falsehood.

No, this picture of human beings and their society cannot be the one God had in mind when breathing His Own Life into the nostrils of the first human being instead of just filling his veins with the right kind of blood. Only God knows how painful it is for me to have had to describe here scenes I never expected to see darkening America's landscape. But that is secularism. The humanity of the secular humanist's conception is definitely not the one our Creator had planned magnificent things for when designing a world so precisely fit to contain life; when fashioning a Creation so complex and so minutely detailed that for it to be a product of happenstance is a physicochemical, mathematical impossibility; when planting sentience in our souls, and eternity in our hearts.

Nature's exactitude in all its grandeur is our omniscient God of Absolutes' personal signature as Creator of all there is, with humanity as the crown of His Creation. The purpose of it all is too sublime to be fully perceived by rebellious minds in a state of denial of God as the Author of life, in refusal of His offer of faith and redemption. For the mind that is dead to

God as Creator is a cinerary urn of meaning, life's significance having become like the ashes of the rebel's burned flag. Such a mind ends up disposing of the dust of devalued human life, while the surviving soul continues the journey to an eternal destination, vainly seeking for life's meaning in arid places where it can never be found.

The real America, the one I and most of my peers remember and love, has been purposely obscured with the passing of time. She's being made to lie, ingloriously, by the wayside of contemporary history's pathway leading to a God-spurning internationalism. Unwittingly or systematically, she is being made to look at the signature of the Author of life written everywhere in nature to have been falsified by ignorance, with this fraudulence only now being detected by the astuteness of scientific knowledge.

Allow this writing to go back to the true America, the humane nation of Olivia's youth, the wholesome America we inherited from Adams, Washington, Lincoln... God.

FOUR

THE NEW COLOSSUS

"Keep, ancient lands, your storied pomp!" cries she
With silent lips. "Give me your tired, your poor,
Your huddled masses yearning to breathe free,
The wretched refuse of your teeming shore.
Send these, the homeless, tempest-tost to me,
I lift my lamp beside the golden door!"
(Emma Lazarus)

"America is prosperous because she is good" (Tocqueville)

Like me, millions of people all over the world have sensed, while still in their own countries, that in America was to be found a natural habitat for the human being; that her Founders must have discovered the right recipe for creating the most favorable circumstances where people could live well and thrive in freedom; that America was a promise of hope to suffering humanity, a promise that she was keeping well; that she was a shelter to people at the mercy of life's distresses.

I was one of them, a small *lump* of the *huddled masses* of the American poet's metaphor, born and raised thousands of miles away in a country known for its tyrannous dictatorship from birth to adulthood. I didn't know then, as I know now, that America's socio-political secret for being different from other nations had to do with the concept of human life - its origin, worth, meaning, and purpose, and God's role in all of this as Creator of *"all there is,"* in the words of the Judeo/ Christian Scriptures.

I have lived in this Country long enough now to verify that that discernment about America as a nation that favored dignifying human life was justified; that those who conceived this Nation had somehow succeeded in discovering the right moral and political ingredients to comprise a healthy atmosphere yielding the proper incentives for productive living. This geopolitical peculiarity has enriched the lives of countless human beings through the years, both here and abroad - even the life of an underprivileged Latino like me born at the edge of a jungle. Not seeking the poetized Shangri-la, and never reaching out, politically, for Utopia, America's Founders correctly identified the features which a citizen-friendly nation should have.

I had yet to learn that the quality of life in a Country, whether good or bad, depends on the concept of human life prevailing in their society - that a nation is defined by how its people define human life. The Fathers of America made sure that her identifying features were accurately prescribed in our Nation's foundational documents, papers which were destined to become historically distinctive and inimitable in the eyes of honest statesmen worldwide. *"The creation of the United States of America is the greatest of all human adventures... Americans originally aimed to build an other-worldly 'City on a Hill', but found themselves designing a republic of the people to be a model for the entire planet"*, wrote Paul Johnson, the trusted British historian, in *A History of the American People*. At the heart of America's success is the historical fact that in creating America, our Founders honored God as Creator.

What they succeeded in doing had never happened in other nations before. Wisely, they carefully articulated in writing the identifying characteristics of the new nation. This precaution made it possible for future Americans to continue producing, breathing, and maintaining the nourishing atmosphere for human life which they had devised.

This exceptionalism of America, which present-day American "progressivists" deny - or are incomprehensibly ashamed of - was a reality to us foreigners. In learning that America was willing to share with the world what she had, many of us were ready to do all we could to come here and savor the blessings which her uniqueness made possible. We discerned her willingness as warm and sincere; we experienced America as a truly humane nation. People from all over our needy world found the door to this auspicious setting to be generously open to deserving knockers. A sincere welcome on the part of her leaders to partake of their Nation's fortunateness awaited them here. Whether seeking shelter from tyranny, or simply yearning for accomplishments difficult or impossible to achieve in our native Countries, millions of us came to America ready to wed our earthly destiny with that of this unique Nation. Some of us died defending her. Some had their children eventually sitting in her Congress, courts, and in the Oval Office, cradle-Americans and Americans By Choice having trusted them with a people-bestowing power, a government system never before experienced in human history.

We were not disappointed with America. This nation has given us more than we expected, more than some of us deserved, even though, unhappily so, too many of us never learned what actually made this Nation what she had become. Until recently, cradle-Americans and Americans By Choice were able to share in this Nation's wealth of blessings just by being here. We obtained a share of her prosperity in proportion to our effort only. We were not required to realize what produced the elements forming the resources making our attainments possible; we only had to make good use of the innate freedom and incentives available here. For a time, her largesse, which also proceeded from these fertile resources, made this realization unnecessary. But today, this is no longer true. Changes have occurred in America of late, making it so that, from now on, to preserve what we have, whether we are cradle Americans or immigrants, depends on our knowing her true identity and doing what is necessary to halt the now accelerated rate of change. Whether we realize it or not, our fortunate way of life and America's true identity are Siamese twins having one heart in common. If we try to separate with our choices and ballots the good things we have in America from her true identity, as our present rebellious elite proposes we do, we'll lose both of them.

It is an observable fact that too many Americans By Choice and later generations of cradle-Americans are blissfully unaware of the ingredients that composed our vigorous national atmosphere, even while partaking of it. Had this not been the case, we would not be seeing our nation distancing herself from her proven steady moorings as she is today. The fast pace of change America has been going through under a governance equally unapprised of her true identity makes that knowledge crucial if we are not to lose forever the America we know and love. The hard truth is that our Nation is right now teetering on the edge of disaster. As planned by un-American Americans, the New Colossus is now unhealthily depressed, morally and economically. This combination of ills has originated from a wrong understanding of America, formed by an erroneous theoretical concept of human life. I can't think of anything deemed wrong in America today that cannot be traced to an understanding of human beings as just another animal "species". This poses a kind of threat never experienced before in our Land. This Nation has gone through many threatening times before, but never anything as dire as this.

All the material and immaterial good in America is not an accident of history, but the fruit of a purposeful planting of the right kind of seeds only found in the greenhouse where faith in a God of Creation grows. In our present socio-political scene, unless we protect and nurture the plants, they shall wither and die. But we can't protect them without knowing their natural habitat which only America's true identity provides. Translated into practical terms, this means that the unfortunate circumstances which many of us immigrants have known so well in our own countries of origin have caught up with us in a nation where we least expected such things to happen. Cradle-Americans may soon be left with their basic needs not met, and Americans By Choice may be left with our hands emptied of what we came here to secure, this time with no hope of filling them again.

We cannot underestimate the urgency with which we must acquaint ourselves with America's true identity and then react and act accordingly. In today's socio-economic and political malaise, only by absorbing, living, and voting guided by a true understanding of who America really is will we be able to retain the good resulting from our nation's valuable uniqueness. Only if enough of us know who America is in reality will we be able to discern whether those seeking to represent us have, indeed, the same knowledge and have proved themselves to be determined to act upon and preserve that knowledge. Unless this happens, and soon, we shall not be capable of governing ourselves as intended by our Founders.

Democracy can quickly become an unwitting channel to tyranny as the majority surrenders its power to politicians equally unaware of America's true identity. If we allow this, as happens in other nations, we shall have to settle for being governed by politicians having nothing in common with us and with the nation we inherited. Not aware themselves of who America truly is and how we came to possess the good things we have, they will certainly mismanage these goods politically and economically. This is happening right now, this time openly. We have already had freedom-quenching laws and obligations foisted on us against our will, in defiance of our people-empowering Constitution. Our present governance is set on taking away from us our freedom, our family, our God, our country. We have practically been forced to be content with less freedom and a lowered quality of life. A Government unlike us, with power *over* us, not *from* us, shall continue to look at our written Constitution as a foundational document to be interpreted and changed in a way to fit an American version of socialism, the foreign ideology it seeks to have us live under.

Then the ultimate political evil will befall us: wanting to retain power without having to depend on the votes of *"know-nothing fundamentalists,"* as Prof. Peter Singer calls those who continue to hold to the fundamental values of America, our politicians shall not hesitate to seek the power they crave from any other possible source, including international power-brokers. When added up, the bill's sum total will be America herself, for the enormity of her debt cannot be paid with lavishly printed money or money borrowed from nations determined to destroy our country. Our leaders haven't heeded the warning given to another Nation whose God and values America's Founders adopted: *"The Lord shall open unto thee his good treasure...to bless all the work of thy hands: and thou shall lend unto many nations, and thou shalt not borrow. And the Lord shall make thee the head, and not the tail...above only... not beneath;* **if** *thou hearken unto the commandments of the Lord thy God..."*

Many of us, immigrants especially, are not aware of the extent, the depth of the cultural war being waged in this Country now for years. And the bone of contention, the golden trophy, is none other than America's soul. Her enemies within and without have been seeking for a long time to do away with our notion of the Pilgrims' America and to build here a nation of their liking. The unwanted changes that already have occurred piecemeal in our nation are the spoils of strategic battles they have already won. The cultural war now seems to be entering a final stage. Whether we realize it or not, ABCers are their strategic recruits today. Those of us who don't know who America truly is are being duped to join politically the ranks of the enemy.

The final war spoil is America herself as a sovereign nation. We must, at any cost, win what is shaping up to be the last battle. If we don't win, cradle-Americans and Americans

By Choice could soon find themselves homeless and prisoners in a despotic nation readied to join a despotic world. The very life of the "New Colossus" is what is now at stake. It is very possible that we are witnessing today the final demise of the Pilgrims' America, along with all the good which we have gained through being born here or through having been adopted as America's children.

World events, and changes guided by foreign socio-political ideologies which have already been secured here by those I call un-American Americans are about to nullify our unique and successful experiment as a "government of the people by the people". Though proven historically to be the best form of government ever devised by the human mind, these auspicious words could soon be read only as a footnote in world history. We could soon be under a sole, unbalanced totalitarian power yet to be named. Our once reassuring tripartite system of people-empowered government, the polity with which the wise Founders of America sought to protect us from tyranny, could be a thing of the past. You and I would have then become *"citizens of the world"*, as our children have been stealthily taught to think of themselves in their schooling now for two or three generations.

Though cradle-Americans are also faced today with the same threat, this book is written primarily to alert ABCers of the urgent need to equip ourselves to do what is required of us to help preserve the America that graciously took us in. Too many of us are unaware of the ill-used forces stemming from a wrong kind of pluralism that are politically stripping this nation of her invaluable uniqueness. It is a political fact that can be surely established today that those who seek to recreate America according to their own interpretation and taste are planning to use us "late-comer pilgrims" to accomplish such a purpose. For them, this is a matter of numbers, of votes, and nothing else. No matter what is being broadcast politically, your good is not their ultimate goal, for socialism seeks to please the society as a whole, not the individual. With this ideology you are just a number, and your individuality can be dispensed with for the sake of the society. That's what secular humanism teaches, since people are just another animal "species". That's a lesson of history we can't afford to forget. Thus, the earnestness with which this book's message must reach the ears and hearts of Americans By Choice.

The dark scenario I have just painted about the landscape of history which we are being conditioned to settle for didn't just originate in my mind. And it is not one built in the minds of eccentrics either - of "kooks", in the epithet used to frighten the people who want to keep America as the Founders' America. It is extremely important that readers realize this. Better minds than mine, more qualified observers than I, have been warning the Nation ever since her Fathers declared her independence that every generation must work to maintain the freedom it inherited. A biased media has practically robbed this generation of our voices, instead of being the means of communicating our concerns, as its charter calls it to do. By taking to themselves the lion's share of freedom of speech still abundant in the Land, it has become a fourth source of power never prescribed by the Nation's Constitution.

The worse thing we can do as we are being pulled into the black hole where the America we love could disappear, is to allow misguided Americans or anti-American Americans to mislabel the scenario I have described. Some of our best conservative political commentators still seem yet to realize that it is those determined to weaken the power of our orthodox understanding of America, and the defense of her we offer, who have turned into "buzz words" terms such as "conspiracy" and "black helicopters". Those things are not parts of the scenario I paint here. Had those commentators been born and raised in a Country with full centralized power held by one man or a military junta, as many of us did, these commentators would respond differently. Had they seen how dictatorships enforce their decrees and pretenses with raw power backed by the press and Courts which they control, they would detect America's enemies' clever verbal and political strategies. We must not forget that Nazism and the Holocaust began with a complying German court. Schooled in un-American ideologies, often well-meaning commentators don't seem to believe their eyes and ears when seeing and hearing what they see and hear today. They are not used to so intense dissimulation. They seem to think that the political creation of debilitating circumstances, as many of us have experienced in our Countries of birth, can never happen in America.

It is crucial today that cradle and late generation Americans By Choice educated here from childhood seek to learn the true facts about America's birth lest they learn too late the dark consequences of what is taking place in America even as this is being written. They must intelligently contest what they have learned about America from fraudulent versions of her history; they must honestly compare what our present elite and media profess with the actual events and values noted in her true records. Unrevised records of history in the writings of unbiased historians are not easy to find nowadays, but they are still available.

FIVE

A LUMP FROM
THE HUDDLED MASSES

"This is my story, this is my song
Praising my Savior all the day long"
(Blind Poet Fanny Crosby)

It is almost impossible to correctly understand the soul of America through the worldview prevailing in Western culture for the last two or three generations and now being widely adopted here. Having been born in a "third world Country" before the Second World War, I invite the reader to come with me to a point of history and to a place where the fog of today's secularism is not as thick, and view from there with me this unique nation called America.

My first impression of America started to form in my childhood as I noticed how most parents in my country reacted when their children asked permission to go to a movie theater. "Is it an American or an European movie?" they asked their young ones. If the answer was "American," their offspring had their blessing; there was no need to ask any further question. French and other European movies were a no-no. Even as a child, I knew what those parents meant with their question - that there was something wholesome about most of America's films.

As I was growing up, this offhandedly learned trait of a distant Land started to create a puzzle in my mind that was to grow in complexity as I matured. I was soon to see America as a mixture of strength and kindness, prosperity and charitableness, peace-loving yet possessing a military might strong enough to deliver other nations from their tyrants. I perceived in America a dignifying attitude toward people, a respect for individuals and their needs, and a reputation for being a Christian Nation, Christianity being the religion given credit for what good she had. Living under a dictatorship where power dispenses with good unless in exchange for more power, that seemed to me an outlandish thing.

I was already then guessing that America's moral tenor stemmed from a right interpretation of life which gave the human being a proper worth and a sound meaning. While studying history in the light of the contemporary world events of my time, especially the then on-going war, I was already suspecting that the European nations would soon have to put together what I called even then, "The Puzzle That is America"; that they would have to learn America's secret on how to handle human life and emulate her if they were to influence for good the Western Civilization which, as we learn from history, Judaism and Christianity had created; that if Europe failed to do this, Western Civilization would eventually crumble under the perennial curse which history indicates as having in time destroyed all others - except that of the Jews, even through centuries of Diaspora.

Today, I have lived long enough to see that not only was my analysis as a child correct, but to witness the moral peculiarity distinguishing America from other nations start to evaporate. After the last World War, her level of existential realism was rising dramatically above her once characteristic moral level, morality having become to her, like everything else, relative and situational. Today, like Europe, she is producing human-degrading movies and magazines and exporting them all over the world. Parents who still care to protect their children's character can no longer use the question about a film's origin as a litmus test. Thus, another riddle was added in my mind concerning the identity of an already puzzling Nation. What could have happened to America since she was first introduced to me in my childhood as a principled Country to cause her to act against the wholesome tenets she once was known to spouse and strengthen her character with? Would her growing world influence eventually harm other nations and invite disrespect or even hate for her?

But it was much later that these questions were to come to the fore. At the time of that youthful divination of mine about what made America different from other Countries, the world was writhing in the pains of the Second World War, a conflict which, I learned, America never wanted to enter; the Pearl Harbor attack forced her to do it. When she finally did enter it, she was to become the main participator and liberator of nations. With her awesome military power America could have from "D-Day" gone on conquering the defeated Countries for herself as other powers did and Russia tried to. Years later, and to this date, German is still Germany's language after the costly Marshall plan initiated the reconstruction of this former enemy's nation and return to it its sovereignty, with the American people who financed the arduously executed plan paying for it. This liberality, though it was Nazi bullets and bombs that killed their children, spoke volumes to me about Americans. And Germany was not an exception. Japanese is still the language of Japan today, and Italians still speak Italian. To me, America was, indeed, a unique, strange nation. All this increased the puzzle's mystery in my young mind already acquainted with history's refrain of conquerors taking all and sometimes even destroying the language of the conquered so as to prove and secure their mastership.

In the aftermath of the war, America was the nation that kept Russia - one of her main, though temporary allies in that bloodiest of all wars - from turning Russian into the official language of tens of other nations, though the "bear" succeeded in that for a while. Since then, the bullhorns of ideologues causing international conflicts kept increasing in numbers, decibels, and efficiency. This renewed clashing of socio-political ideologies confirmed my suspicion that the correct solution to the American puzzle was becoming a sine qua non condition for the survival of the Western civilization. I went even further by thinking that the answer to the puzzle could someday be the salvation of the world, if that were possible. That supposition of mine is now filed away in my mind as inconclusive - even if America had been given that role, her becoming enamored with her enemies' political philosophies, as she is now, is changing that possible role into one of a villain. Will America continue to influence the world with what is left of good in her, or will the world invalidate her influence, with history calling her bluff?

After the war, the blossoms of America's uniqueness were turning into abundant fruits. As her world influence and riches grew, so did my conjecture about the role America had the potential to play for good in the life of our Western Civilization. But I knew that to do this she would have to keep herself from whatever had been eroding the civilizing strength of Europe. I was myself unsure then as to what was actually undermining the Old World. As she did when first becoming a new nation, America would have to interpret correctly the emerging socio-political European thought now plunging her into secularism. And America would have to do this even while keeping on the armor of her uniqueness, whatever material it was made from. America had already dealt with political and socio-moral toxins in her youth, like she did with her ghastly human venom of slavery - and, that, at a terrible cost, though she could only take care of herself then. I had hoped that, now mature and fulfilled, she would keep in her consciousness what had enabled the enviable status she had reached as a nation and see that her prestige and its cause influenced the world for good. But I still had yet to find America's actual secret of success, what formed that atmosphere I described as the natural habitat for human beings to live and thrive in peace and prosperity.

With The Puzzle That is America in mind, I did my best to learn her language. Eventually I was to learn about the historical facts of her birth distinguishing her, in the language in which they were written. My passion for words was a great help in this. From what I was learning I could easily picture myself living, raising a family, and dying as an American By Choice, though the possibility of this happening was then vastly remote. It would be years before my search for America's secret didn't have to stop at her borders. When finding myself in America, first as a student and later married to a cradle American, I was able to study in loco the events and circumstances surrounding her unique birth against the backdrop of what I perceived was happening then in her domestic life.

I learned, while here, what every race of people living in this country today needs to - no, must - know: how one shouldn't expect this Nation to accommodate in a short number of years human beings from a hundred different backgrounds and cultures into the uniqueness of America; that to accomplish this is not as simple as the work of a shepherd leading his sheep to greener pastures. While living here, I learned of both good and bad past and current events and circumstances handled by most of her leaders in the light of America's steadying principles and desired values recorded in her Constitution, a document of fundamental laws on governance that has yet to be bettered in the history of humanity. Seeing its principles still practically adhered to was an enormous plus in helping me learn further about America's identity. But the complicated puzzle of America was still incomplete even after settling here and getting married to a true American of Western European extraction. I still needed to acquaint myself fully with America's soul.

While still in my Country of birth, my adolescent eyes saw the pieces of human life's own puzzle spread on the desk of my mind, and that of America still more mysterious than ever in the feverishness of the post-war years. But even with all that murkiness of unpleasant past and present reality for background, I continued to read everything I could find about this unique nation formed by a group of "dissident" Europeans escaping from the secular enclosures of religious tyranny. I was interested in learning about the Pilgrims and Founders just as people with their individual beliefs and way of life. I suspected that America's secret was their secret. Reading only history books written long, long ago and then collecting dust in our local library, I learned that they were steeped in the Judeo/Christian Holy Scriptures. I took to the Bible too. But, again, you can't find a book that presents more puzzles than the Bible for its amalgam of violence and candor, raw justice and love-and-mercy - a book in which you learn of a God Who is both ruthless and loving, a dichotomy easily beyond human comprehension, presiding over an obvious heavenly Heaven and a hellish Hell, whose tokens of self-existence color and discolor our lives as we try to navigate through a sea of good and evil.

I was to find out, after diligently studying the Judeo/Christian Scriptures, that this book is, in reality, not a recipe of placebos for philosophical researchers, but a surgeon's scalpel, a "two-edged sword" as it describes itself. I learned that the Pilgrims were Christians, of the kind the local missionary challenged us to become. I was filtering their Gospel, as I understood it then, through the Chapters of history variously titled "Crusades", "Inquisitions", and "Reforms", religious movements where the lack of humaneness made a mock of Godliness. In the sieves I found as much dregs of diabolic human tortures and barbaric killings in Christendom as in the Chapters titled "Jihads". My conclusion was that the bloodshed was due to a theology that failed to elevate the value and meaning of human life; that their doctrines, even those considered as sound by most, spelled out only a juridical interpretation of righteousness not humane enough to make the long journey from the head to the heart. They were still the rash, though appropriate, Old Testament laws of absolute Justice of a divine standard and not those of the New Testament which spoke of a loving Incarnate God dignifying the worthiness and meaning of people's physicality for its harboring an eternal soul. They were not tempered with the due prizing of human life being so much more than just another animal "species".

From all this, I deduced that there had to be more than religion in America's recipe - as the word "religion" is defined in dictionaries - for the natural habitat for humans which it had created. Republicanism and capitalism alone could not be it either, these being but economic and political formats not addressing the needs of the human soul. Even sweet-sounding democracy couldn't be the answer either, since it can easily bring about tyranny by a majority in the absence of that active ingredient I looked for in America's make-up.

At the time those thoughts were germinating in my mind as a youngster, the world had just experienced the bloody tragedy of the Second World War - obviously, a result of man-centered and God-ignoring ideologies. Being a teenager when the world was just walking out of pools of human blood was a challenging time for a young, feverish mind to be seeking to understand life, let alone trying to solve the puzzle about a distant land. While I was growing up in my Country of birth, a German philosopher had already notified the world that the God Whom the local American missionary named as my Creator, had died. France, still reeling under her guillotine-happy Revolution that produced much blood and little *liberte'* and, of late, Nazism's atrocities, was now plunging herself into existentialism and sharing it with the world through her literary skill. Hiroshima and Nagasaki, with people-decimating, made-in-America mushroom clouds of death in the Japanese sky, were making this nation's identity more complex than I thought.

At that time, the missionary's interpretation of the Savior of humanity - the Pilgrims' *Gospel* - was already becoming more like that of a social activist militating under the banner of a socialist God. It wasn't easy for me and for many of my peers living under a dictatorship to resist the dialectics of ideologues like Hegel and Marx. I would have yielded to them where it not for Communist leaders like Stalin and the millions of human deaths he was then showing to be the cost involved in the application of their political programs. The mystery of human life, its origin and meaning, seemed to me more and more every day to be the greatest of all puzzles, the "mother" of them all - and if so, the Rosetta Stone to deciphering the hieroglyphics of political and religious reality; in short, all of human reality. I knew then that I would have to tackle this enigma alongside my "Puzzle That is America". To do this, I read everything I could find about both human life and that faraway nation that constantly reminded me of herself even in the poverty of my environment.

Had life's Creator given His human creatures the responsibility of defining life by themselves? And who is to do it, scientists, theologians or politicians? I guessed that a religious Englishman named Charles Darwin must have already asked this question long before I did. But he was just a scientist who seemed to have only dabbled in religion, and he left the question unanswered both theologically and philosophically, while his theory on the genesis of life, nevertheless, changed forever the world we have to live in. After returning from the wilderness of South America, he promptly "notarized the certificate of the divine death" being pronounced in Europe with his *On the Origin of Species*. Happily for me, even as a child I refused to think of a monkey as my father or brother. I knew myself as too much of a human being for that. In my incipient logic, I concluded that if I had a monkey for an ancestor, I really shouldn't be seeing siblings of mine jumping from tree to tree in the South American jungle I was familiar with. They would be long-buried with the genes of their own ancestors. To put it in the colorful idiom of the language I was teaching myself then, I was already past my childish desire to jump about, to "monkey around". I would have to study evolution further to see how Mr. Darwin explained this. And in King's English, too.

That Englishman's theory on the origin of life not only changed the world, but by cheapening the worth of human beings in cataloguing them as a mere animal species he made it the poorest currency with which to purchase worthless political changes. I suspect that with his theory, that scientist took the first step to cause the sun to go down on the British Empire on which it was said at the time that it never set. Thoughts like these would immediately make me think of America. This, because it's evident not only that Darwin's theory of humanity's origin facilitated the barbarities of Nazism, Communism, eugenics, and abortion, with the multimillion deaths they have produced, but also that the low valuation of human life which Darwinism suggests could yet do away with America before I could get acquainted with her soul.

With the Second World War, meaningfulness confirmed for me the place Reason has in the battle for truths. Did the few samples of humanity sailing on a ship with the romantic name of "Mayflower", people who had yet no way of knowing what their Bible really meant when stating that *the life is in the blood*, know something about life they didn't yet have the vocabulary to express? George Washington himself died after being "bloodletted" to cure what could have been just a bad cold even though his well-used Bible lay by his bedside. Did a nation called America succeed in expressing life's true meaning in terms of national polity, the way God chose another nation, that of another pilgrim people, the Jews, to reveal Himself to humankind as The Way, the Truth and the *Life* in the ruthlessness of His absolute justice and, later, in the incomprehensible demonstration of His love? Could that be the explanation as to why today the religion of an unincarnated, unredeeming Islamic god has both nations, America and Israel, in the crosshairs of murderous weapons sanctioned by their divinity to be used in conquering Western Civilization "religiously"?

It would be years before such questions could be intelligently asked by this small lump of humanity daring today to write a book about a nation now foolishly divesting herself of her glory as leaders and academics hazardously link her orthodox paradigm with that of a hate-filled fundamentalism of America's avowed enemies. Today, the crucial need for the right answers to the questions of my youth is being evidenced by the daily headlines and prurient sights we see everywhere at a time when Truth is no longer to be written with a capital "T". Yet, Truth alone, absolute in the exclusivity of its definition, has the key to life's meaning and human freedom. The situational morality of well-educated, modern secularists, coupled with relativism, keep our frontiers open for the evils through which God-ignoring ideologies threaten to come and enslave us all. And this time there is no New World left where a freedom-seeking America could sail to and there repeat herself.

SIX

A 2OTH CENTURY PILGRIM IN A SECULARIZING AMERICA

"All things were made by Him [God] *...In Him was life."*
(Gospel by John)

"And even as they did not like to retain God in their knowledge, God gave them over to a reprobate mind, to do those things which are not convenient." (Apostle Paul)

"... every man did what was right in his own eyes" (Moses)

I took my first steps on American soil in New York's International Airport, then called Idlewild. The next ones were taken in a bus filled with foreigners like myself, bound for Manhattan, where people from every Country on the globe were already living. That happened in the Fifties. The discrepancy I noticed between what for so long I looked forward to seeing and what I first saw showed me that the atmosphere of that American ideal human habitat was going stale. Now I had to find out not only what actually had formed the pristine atmosphere which I was still assured existed, but I also had to discover what was polluting it. I quickly realized that to find the soul of America in New York City would be like finding the famous needle in a haystack; to discover here the true meaning of life would be even more difficult.

The discolored American ethos I found in the cities of America, coming, as I guessed, from the negative values then present and the positive ones lacking, in the unwholesomeness of their atmosphere were already palpable. My initial understanding of America arrived at from my first, adolescent impression of the once faraway Nation clashed roundly with what I was seeing now in Times Square and Wall Street. I found Times Square not a place for Pilgrims to frequent; and Wall Street offered no lure to Puritans either. America's life as viewed in a big city discomfited this foreign student.

While participating in the life of my hostess Nation, I noticed indications that the unhealthy atmospheric condition of American big cities would be inexorably spreading to the manicured countryside and peaceful looking towns of the Nation's hinterlands. For either due to sophistication or credulity, big, cultured cities are natural models of mores and standards for the rest of the country. The proliferating, willing media would see to that. The insidious, magical way with which television was soon to visually teach those mores in living color was to prove me right.

Now as a member of the generational trend-setting group of people called Student Class, I had a front seat in the theater where the drama of American life was progressing. That's when I saw and heard what I couldn't from afar, in the scenes and plots reflecting what was actually happening with and in America's soul. It was while partaking of the life of Colleges and Universities that I realized how deeply the American culture was being affected by the secularism and existentialism which I had already perceived as being rooted in European atheistic philosophies. Its scenery took the colors of the naturalistic explanation of life's origin which spawned a movement already on its way to becoming a religion - secular humanism. The Judeo/Christian Holy Scripture informs us that at the beginning of human history, the Father of Lies proclaimed the First Great Lie about God and humanity: *"ye shall not surely die* [as God told you, for rebelling against Him], *He knows... that your eyes shall be opened, and ye shall be as gods, knowing good and evil"*. After millennia of human suffering and death which demonstrated his First Lie as a lie indeed, a Second Lie, naturalism, was announced in an unholy "scripture" - the Humanist Manifesto - this time with the full endorsement of science. By its content, it's evident that this Second Lie is being told to cover up the consequences of the first one. As happened in Europe, human culture was giving this nation a choice whether to believe that life just happened like "fogus fatus" in a swamp, or that it was conceived in God's heart and birthed through His holy breath. America's academia chose the first and has been teaching the same heresy to the American people now for years. It seems that America has opted to continue believing both lies, and her once vibrant soul has been pining ever since.

I was astonished to find out how much that oldest of religions where selfhood is worshipped had taken hold of American culture. Today, for all practical purposes, secular humanism is the predominant religion in America, though often in garb of traditional religions. Not until actually studying and living in America could I have realized how a religious-political-philosophic proclamation few Americans ever heard about or read, first written over one hundred years ago and signed by a handful of people, had been changing America. Two more manifestoes reemphasizing their message were written since then, the last one in celebration of the year 2.000, and this time signed by thousands. This tells us that as the number of signers has increased, so also has the new religion which is changing America almost beyond recognition.

The anti-American academia's audacity in proclaiming to the Nation in writing what they stood for, a clear antithesis of America's foundational values, was understandable - freedom of speech in America was abundant and still practically considered a sacred thing. But I learned that Secular Humanists proceeded immediately to corrode this country's foundation through their heretical dogmas with hardly a resisting effort by the nation. They did this mostly by taking charge of the Nation's school system from kindergartens to Universities.

Through textbooks and lectures they expertly conditioned the new generations of leaders and voters to abandon the orthodox beliefs and values of the Fathers of America. Before long, the whole Country became, unwarily, a meeting-room for seminars on humanistic doctrines. Their converts were numerous enough to effect changes in America's culture, way of life, and politics.

The following quotation from the first of those significant documents summarizes well the religious dogmas now replacing this Nation's Judeo/Christian fundamental tenets that distinguished America from other nations. I find it also an appropriate looking glass to use in order to see what has been happening to America and a telescope to view what her future may well be like. Today, it seems that all areas of life in America are affected by these rebellious words. Some of the changes they effected have already been made permanent:

"Religious Humanists regard the universe as self-existing and not created... the traditional dualism of mind and soul must be rejected... Humanism asserts that the nature of the universe depicted by modern mind makes unacceptable any supernatural or cosmic guarantees of human values... religions that place revelation, God, ritual, or creed above human needs and experience do a disservice to the human species... We find insufficient evidence for belief in the existence of the supernatural; it is either meaningless or irrelevant to the question of the survival and fulfillment of the human race. As non-deists, we begin with humans, not God, nature, not deity... No deity will save us, we must save ourselves." (The Humanist Manifesto I).

Few parents realized how determined these anti-American Americans were, in their own words, *"to change the way Americans think"* by controlling their children's education. Even today, few of them are familiar with the secular humanists' last Century battle cry launching the campaign to use our children's schools for secular indoctrination. In a lecture at a teachers' seminar in 1973 a professor of Education and Psychiatry at Harvard University, typifies the significance of that battle cry. Like with other leading educators, this professor minced no words:

"Every child in America entering school at the age of five is mentally ill because he comes to school with certain allegiances toward our founding fathers, toward our elected officials, toward his parents, toward a belief in a supernatural Being, toward the sovereignty of this nation as a separate entity. It is up to you, teachers, to make all of these sick children well by creating the international children of the future." This demonstration of so radical departure from our Nation's basic values, coming from Harvard University, a school once established to teach Judeo/Christian principles, is very revealing. Pronounced first in 1973, this professor's words were reaffirmed in 1983 during other childhood education seminars. They accurately represented the views of influential secular humanists of the time. These views, stealthily implemented in textbook material since they were taught to teachers tell the story of how America was to shed her true identity.

You almost have to be a foreigner just being introduced to American life to be able to identify this Nation's unexpected lowering of moral standards and its adoption of un-American values as being a direct consequence of two generations having been schooled in secular humanism. Today, our generation of television viewers can hardly realize the import of a journalist presiding over a debate between political candidates mockingly waving a Bible in the air and asking the contestants, who among them still believed in what it taught. Not enough Americans fear for their Nation when learning of someone like Dr. Singer promoting abortion and eugenics as a professor in charge of the Department of Ethics of a school originally established to teach Judeo/Christian values. It doesn't disturb them much when this scholar goes so far as to campaign for the legality of killing a baby during the first thirty days from its birth; they have been made unable to connect this diabolical "ethics" with the awakening monster of Nazi eugenics now operating within our border with the blessings of our government. It is a frightening thing to find how the conscience of a generation of once humane people has been conditioned through education to accept the barbarism of fifty million babies so far being killed in their mothers' wombs with our court's approval - a generation made to forget that the savagery of the Nazi Holocaust began with a complying German Court.

The connection between secular humanistic thought being taken in by the nation and the changes America has been going through is unmistakable. When I first came to America, the popular musical taste was already descending from the enchantment of sublimity to the rhythmic pulsating of flesh and sensuality. It all started naively enough with a generation inured to the danger of flirting with a taste for what is new, without identifying where and what it can lead to. Since then, this inerrant evaluator of a nation's culture has been widely indicating the symptoms of cultural decay, with the syncopated frenzy of its music keeping up with the accelerating pace of life. The tempo seemed to tell that there was no time to wait for answers to life which could never come in the new secular setting; after all, the new generation was taught by the changing culture that when you are dead, you are dead, and that was it. One has to cram as many gratifications into life as sensuality can take. I knew then why the ancient philosopher could write, "let me teach a nation what to sing and I'll conquer it." With its plunge in tempo, popular music was already on its way to crash and disintegrate against the hard-core rebelliousness of the "rap music" of death now disrupting the symphony of life. This innovation would soon be denying people the folksy means of pleasurable expressions which only melody and harmony can provide.

In the visual arts, it was considered more sophisticated to disregard that important point of reference outside the canvas which gives the proper shape and credibility to the thing or scenery pictured. The resulting amorphous representation was, in a coy stance, not meant to show the beauty found, since no truth exists on its own, but only as the individual artist thought or just felt about it. Art was to be used as another tool to make personal or political statements, even if obscure or shocking. As the religion of secular humanism's icon, the person of the artist was to express self and the culture producing its view, even if in an aberrant, illogical way.

In literature, the most popular works were those which depicted scenes of stark reality with wording that graphically resonated with that visible reality of human bodies as being all that there is, only temporarily alive on the world stage where they were placed by a mere accident of nature. The latest psychological theories were already attempting to explain away the transcendental yearnings of the soul. The concept of an eternal human soul was considered as fictional a thing as the people imagined by the writers and the plots construed with them. Being young then, had I not been looking up instead of at my own navel as secular humanism suggests in its existentialism, I would have probably joined the hippy crowd on my way to meet with meaninglessness and spiritual death. I would have been hobnobbing with other young people then seeking for answers about life's meaning solely in the beauty of withering flowers and evanescent enchantments and finding them discolored and lackluster; not reaching enough fulfillment, I would have been settling for consolation in the oblivion offered by hallucinogens and the narcotic incense offered before the dissatisfying tepidity of "free love".

Though with an unsure voice which was never to become convincing, evolution was making those questions about life seem superfluous. The spontaneity of life's appearance on earth, as it guessed, negated a Creator God even with the statement of unbelief not openly articulated. The answers to those questions about life's meaning and purpose were no longer considered crucial to individuals and nations. Textbooks and treatises on Biology, Philosophy, and Psychology were defiantly attempting to invalidate the now allegedly discredited Judeo-Christian teachings. A wide acceptance of an unproved scientific theory of life's origin was causing more and more Americans to look down and out, not up and within.

A single false alarm about the origin of life and its finality at death, the naturalism that gave birth to secular humanism, was enough to produce all these soul-destroying changes. Life being lived by one's own perishable senses was all that mattered. The deification of selfhood was being confirmed to the ears and heart of a Nation wealthy enough to bring to it the richest of oblations. With that lowering of the eyes to the yet unredeemed mother earth alone, the meaningfulness-building purpose for life became a pariah in human thinking. Existentialism, a philosophy of life already dominating European thinking and life style for a number of years, was fast becoming a way of life here too, and thriving, as everything in this Nation does in its abundance of freedom and means.

It was to this changing cultural scenario that this foreign student from a "third world Country" came, looking up to America, the wise mother that he thought she was, still searching for the meaning and purpose of life. My questions were now lost in the midst of proliferating secular props which catered mostly to the flesh and its pleasures. I had to dig further and deeper to find what I was looking for. For pick and shovel, all I had was a classical, pre-nihilism philosophy and a smattering of Bible verses learned as a child.

While trying to adjust to life in a nation becoming so dissimilar to the template I brought with me, I was still grappling with the Puzzle That is America. I was more fascinated now with the idea of a country claiming to having been established on *"True Religion"*, terminology her Founders never tired of using and whose original meaning seemed lost in the fog of the Nation's history. It was becoming evident to me that the adoption of a divine program by the Founders of America to insert meaning and purpose into human and national life was the main thread in the mesh of her history. This feature which had so characterized America in its early years had suddenly become an occasion for stumbling for most Americans in this once spiritually driven Nation, especially among her growing elite.

As a young foreign student just arriving in America, and as a pursuer of meaning and purpose for my own life, I saw thinking Americans collecting answers about life in the halls of Science and labs, and though finding them dubious, still insisting on living by them. The answers to life's questions, if available and necessary for living, were supposed to be found there, and not in churches or synagogues, those institutions now taken for innocuous additions to a culture, like the appendix was thought to be to the human body. Though religious, too many citizens of this Nation where the majority of her people determines her choices, were deciding not to abide by what her Fathers' Gospel taught in the schools they started. God and Creation, the main part of the syllabus, were now considered myths for lack of "scientific proofs ". These subjects were no longer to be taught in schools, only mentioned in passing, if at all. If present in a school library, what the Nation's Fathers called The Holy Scriptures was to be left, unopened, on the Literature Section shelf. The theories of *The Origin of Species* were to replace the truths of the Bible. The people's and the nation's life were to be lived willfully disconnected from the Creator of Life. This strategy of America's deceivers prompted me to do what modern Americans were being told not to do - I began again to earnestly study the Judeo/Christian Holy Scriptures. I read the Bible through probingly, several times. I was to find out later that that was the best thing I have ever done, for this eventually led me to solve the two puzzles I had long grappled with - The Puzzle That Is America and The Puzzle That is Life.

And I was about to find the needle in the haystack.

SEVEN

THE THREEFOLD CORD

"... a threefold cord is not quickly broken." (Ecclesiastes)

"Our ancestors established their system of government on morality and religious sentiment. Moral habits, they believed, cannot safely be trusted on any other foundation than religious principle, nor any government be secure which is not supported by moral habits."
(Daniel Webster)

"[W]e have no government armed with power capable of contending with human passions unbridled by morality and [the true] *religion. Avarice, ambition, revenge, or gallantry, would break the strongest cords of our Constitution as a whale goes through a net. Our Constitution was made only for a moral and religious people. It is wholly inadequate to the government of any other."* (John Adams)

Once upon a time there was a group of influential thinkers who knew that their Western World owed its success to a culture that was initially formed by a belief in God. They were fugitives from a dominant country where the governing power was exercised through both politics and religion, a partnership which has always produced human tragedies in the form of persecutions, tortures, and killings, in the name of both politics and religion.

When, in the course of events, this people needed to form their own nation, they envisioned a governmental power issuing from the people and not from a self-centered and often cruel elite, or *gentility*, as the governing class of their time was called. This form of government was never successfully tried before anywhere in the world. They knew that such a unique experiment in government had to take place in an environment of moral values which only spirituality can create, or it would fail; theirs would be a polity that welcomed God in the affairs of the new Country. But *God* has always meant religion in every human culture, and they already knew that religion and politics could not mingle together without the usual loss of people's freedom, dignity, and even life itself once religion turned into religionism and shared the seat of power with politics. They realized that for their experiment in government to produce the results they expected, they would have to keep those two forces consciously connected but apart - like in a marriage, where both husband and wife produce children out of the closest of their union while still remaining two distinct individuals living together peacefully and productively.

The leaders of the people succeeded in their project beyond their expectations. They did this by inserting in their nation's founding documents insights only found in a book whose teaching steered their thinking, a book which dealt realistically with the subject of God, Nature, and human beings. They trusted this book because the knowledge it revealed, though for a time often refuted by science, has through the centuries always been found to be correct once science's newly discovery laws of nature confirmed the factuality of what was once contested. That fact the history of science dutifully documents. Those leaders had also noted that the hundreds of predictions about historical world events found in this Book were fulfilled throughout the years in their smallest details, despite the numerical impossibility of this happening as attested by the laws of mathematics.

Anyone in our Country who has not been deceived by secular humanism's worldview knows immediately that this is not a fable; that the new nation was America and the book was the Judeo/ Christian Scriptures. Historians have to acknowledge that America's Fathers did indeed weave a belief in the Judeo/Christian God into the fabric of the nation they founded. Atheists and agnostics can decry this truth or try to minimize its role in the formation of this Country's identity, but they can't deny what America's Founders did.

The twentieth Century Pilgrim writing this book never doubted for a moment the fact of God's existence and of this Nation's Fathers welcoming this reality into the birthing of their Country. I had studied the same Book that inspired America's conception long and hard enough to know that God, its true Author, never failed to deliver what He promised - in this case, of keeping the new Nation free and strong, with the sustaining strength of the biblical threefold cord. *"God's Providence"*, the Founders called that keeping power. I knew that the cord was strong enough to hold America securely in spite of the ever increasing weight of her growing greatness. I knew also that these truths would eventually lead me to the secret of America's success as a nation. But I suspected that there was more to it than a belief in the God historically believed in in common with other Countries.

Since partaking myself of the life of this nation, I kept seeing her floundering perilously through the years, frantically trying to remain herself. At the beginning, I didn't worry much, as I rested in the assurance that America had been designed with the ability to last to the end of time, if her children so desired, an assurance I shared with such luminaries as Washington and Lincoln. The *"Light on a Hill"* was to never go off. I knew that she was being held by a threefold cord which her Founders had secured in God. What I was yet to discover was that the unbreakable threefold cord holding up America was the Triune Judeo/Christian God Himself Whom the Holy Scriptures quote as saying at the beginning of human existence:*"let **Us** make Man."* The actual three strands I was later to understand as being Creation, Redemption, and Sustenance, the offices God executes in his gracious manifestation of Himself to individuals and nations choosing to be under God.

The unique vision of the Founders of America to marry governance with true spirituality - God, neither spouse dominating the other, lasted long enough to foster America's growth into the greatness she has reached. But like a runner's stamina that weakens under the laws of nature as the athlete races to the finish-line, the force of those provisions abated through the years under the laws of fallen human nature. As scientific knowledge increased, lured by this new source of power, the elitism dormant in people living under such promising conditions didn't remain inactive. By the last Century, some leaders became self-assured enough to practically and politically disown the Pilgrims' and Founders' Judeo/Christian God as the source of America's exceptionalism and successes that characterized her from the beginning and vouchsafed her greatness. They took this disastrous step when they allowed themselves to be led by the creeds of secular humanism which naturalism dictated - no God, no Creation, no absolute moral standard, no national individuality. Since then, the doctrines of un-American political ideologies are being gradually, stealthily, being written into the laws of our Land. Today, after years of cultural and political pounding on America's foundation with the hammer of skepticism, we find ourselves facing a strong possibility that her experiment in people's self-government and all that makes her unique and great is about to fail. And with the failure the Founders' America will certainly cease to exist.

America's solidly built foundation started to crumble when secular humanism's philosophical and political beliefs became a religion in our leaders' minds and literature, with precepts premised not on God and spirituality, but on socio-political activities only secularly driven. The Nation's governing elite took for her a paramour and abandoned her spouse. Enamored with their secular religion's dogmas, our leaders have been gradually enlarging and deifying Government while de facto taking away from the people the reins of governmental power. The academia is bringing down their imagined "wall of separation between State and Religion" and linking government with the religion of secular humanism. Ironically, the strategy they used was to allege that America was becoming a theocracy and should be made free from religious influence. As has always happened in God-spurning nations, an increasingly oppressive government is ready here to team up with the repressive religion of secularism to change this Country into a nation befitting their God-denying beliefs. America is now experiencing tyranny for the first time in our Nation's history. So far, the tyranny we have been experiencing is a "soft tyranny", as some of today's political commentators describe our present political atmosphere. But history is there to warn us that that's how all hard tyrannies start.

What is happening to America now once happened to the other country whose steps the Pilgrims wanted to follow when conceiving America, as they themselves professed in writing - the Jewish nation, a people who were initially content with having their national affairs be guided by God's laws and moral standard. We learn about the "change" the Israelites sought from the pages of the Holy Scriptures: *"Then the elders of Israel... came to Samuel...* [the custodian of Israelite spirituality at the time] *and said unto him, Behold, thou art old, and thy sons walk not in thy ways: now make us a king to judge us like all other nations."* That is our America today. American academia and her political elite are being convinced that their nation needs to fundamentally change, rather than keep that which has so far worked miracles for our Nation. Today, we are mostly being governed by a class of people, in all three constituted sources of power, who have no place in a people-governed Republic - leaders not truly representing the peoples' beliefs and choices made under the fear of God. Like the Israelites of old, they are turning their backs on the God of Moses and Samuel, the Pilgrims' God, and leading the people away from Him and His ways. They want our historically exceptional nation to be like all the other nations. In America's case, with today's increasing progress of science and human pride, God is being neglected not only as the God Who revealed Himself to the world through the Jewish people - the God Who is *"above all gods"* - but as Creator of *"all there is,"* especially humanity.

With the present believable threat of fatal political storms powerful enough to destroy America, there is a rush by God-believing Americans to come up with the reasons why the threefold cord seems to be fraying, and apparently becoming progressively weaker; to identify the strand - or strands - in the cord needing strengthening, or even replacement. They approach the problem as being of a political nature. But God, Who is Himself America's threefold cord, is not only not easily broken but is not breakable. What is really threatening America of demise today is that to too many Americans, their God is no longer the God Whom our Fathers knew and whose existence their founding documents acknowledge. Our Nation's present God is not the God of the Bible. Our culture has been polluting His identity in people's minds, the same way America's identity is being polluted. This backsliding has to do with the origin of life, especially human life, its worth, meaning and meaningfulness which were wisely considered by our Nation's Fathers when conceiving America. Our Founders' God is now being denied His identity as Creator of life. This rebellion against God as our Creator is tantamount to atheism - the true irreligion as opposed to our Founders' *"True Religion"*- which America's Fathers had determined as her future destroyer if allowed into her culture. Naturalism has replaced the Pilgrims' God with a god or gods and this heresy has since become America's Achilles' Heel. This unfortunate replacement has disturbed our understanding of reality to the point of having many of our once sensible citizens looking up to the State as god, and to "entitlements" as dues its human icons. The Founders' *"God's Providence"* was no longer available and this placed people and Nation at the mercy of a good without God, a good no longer to be worked for, but expected from the god of statism.

Today, the marriage of governance with spirituality is being hastily dissolved. America, together with our Western Civilization, is dangling above the abyss that has swallowed previous nations and civilizations. And our leaders are foolishly, tragically, letting go of the threefold cord.

EIGHT

THE PUZZLE THAT IS LIFE

"In Him [God Incarnate] *was life; and the life was the light of men"*. (John's Gospel)

After all the years since it happened, my wife still talks about a moving experience she had when our daughter was born. To this day Olivia relives the reverence of that moment whenever it comes to her mind. She tells me that when our baby was first placed in her arms after the birth, the little thing promptly fixed her eyes on those of her mother and kept them there for a long time, seemingly on purpose. No sounds or movements accompanied the steady gaze coming from the tiny body just entering the earth's atmosphere. As she looked back at those innocent eyes Olivia was guessing in them questions about life of which we only become aware at the dawn of our reasoning. "Okay, mommy," they seemed to say to her, "so you are one of the human beings responsible for escorting me out of the mysterious world of non-being. You were one of the parties willing me into the world of the living. Please, please, tell me, what is life all about? I must know. What kind of place is this world I am to live in? Who am I? Who are you? What are we here for? Where do we go from here?"

Indelible, unremitting questions.

"Madman, nobody can define life; just limit yourself to living", a disconsolate poet wrote long before Sartre preached existentialism. I know today that this poet, a compatriot of mine, was dead wrong. But our natural tendency is to quickly agree with him and, like millions of other people, proceed to do exactly what he suggests - just keep on living even if meaninglessly or with false, unhealthy meaning for greed. Yet, the correct answers can be learned and applied to the life of people and nations. Though she insists on forgetting, this has been historically demonstrated by America.

I had lived with our Susie's questions unanswered since my early youth. Like most people, I had accepted the commonly shared conclusion that these questions are among many others that people go to their graves without being able to answer. Today, I realize how extremely costly and consequential such a conclusion has been to people and nations since the beginning of history for lack of timely answers.

It is a fact that most of us think that it is not necessary that we personally define life. As when we turn the light on in a dark room a thousand times without knowing or having to ask what electricity is, probably most of us feel no need to know for sure what life is all about. That is a risky thing to do because how a people live - or die - depends mostly on the philosophy of influential thinkers, on their nation's culture, and on the kind of government and polity these forces devise.

Nations' leaders, their interpretation of human life, and the culture producing both of them determine the kind of life most of their people live. They shape the way people relate to themselves, to others, to God, to things, to reality itself. They mold, by and large, the tenor of people's and their nation's life. They shape the conditions of living. They can influence one's emotional and physical health. They design people's culture and politics until the age following it changes or destroys them. They can prolong life or shorten it. They edit the narrative of human history. Countless millions have died premature and, too often, agonizing deaths because of an elite's conception of human life that minimizes its worth and dignity. This is true whether the age people live in is called the Age of Reason, the Atomic Age, or the Technological Age.

An awareness of this syndrome as one of the producers of human suffering and untimely death is highly needed to understand history. Civilizations have risen and fallen under the power of this recurring pattern. Besides the multitude of people decimated by wars, political and religious misinterpreters of human life have often, purposely and cruelly, taken the lives of millions of peoples at will. History has called the life philosophy of the first group of life-interpreters Communism, Nazism and other forms of despotic government, mostly atheistic. The second group comprise religious movements also ignoring or discounting the worth of human beings, even before naturalism and Darwinism robbed human life of its worth. These have been called Crusades, Inquisitions, Jihads, Reforms.

It is a sobering thing to realize that the perception of life's worth as low, its richness and purpose ignored or denied, has always been more of a threat to human existence than nature's cataclysms. More deaths have been caused by the atheistic and religious cruelty of man to man than all of nature's catastrophes combined - except, probably The Great Flood reported by the Bible.

Mostly because of the theory of evolution which science has accepted as truth a priori, the last Century turned out to be the bloodiest period in human history. Yet, that theory remains to this date just that - a human theory. And the reason for the horrid statistics which have resulted ever since is, basically, the cheapening of human life which naturalism ascertains. It is sheer madness for Americans to allow our laws, our values, and our way of life to be premised by a man-made philosophy of life based on a unproved theory lasting as a so-called truth for over a century and a half.

Today, as citizens and voters, the American people cannot afford not to discover by themselves the true origin of life, if we are to continue to be safe and free. The alternative is to submit to the modus vivendi being designed by a growing elite with its un-American understanding of life. The ignoring of life's meaning and worth which has enfeebled other nations has now started to turn many of us into self-delusional existentialists and willing wards of the State. Because of this, we can hardly call ourselves a self-governing people anymore.

In the present political turmoil, we the people, living in a once human life-dignifying Nation, now find ourselves in a position of having no choice but to learn by ourselves what is true about life with all its worth and promises, to believe it, live by it, and see to it that those we allow to have power over us do the same. The extant theory on the origin of life never dignified the human being and it never will. Contrary to evolutionist doctrines, the rebelliousness of human nature is not evolving into something good and favorable to human life since Adam's first rebelled against the Creator God after believing the First Lie. If our Nation's spiritual and moral deterioration resulting from a false understanding of life is not stopped by discrediting naturalism, human existence, especially that of the unborn, the old, the feeble, and the unwanted, will continue to be threatened. History shall continue to repeat itself, her chapters to be still written with human blood; and with a technology advanced as never before, we could yet be seeing the whole human civilization decimated, possibly within minutes. The medieval swords and the clubs of barbarians killed one individual at a time. Machine guns kill thousands in minutes. A modern bomb can kill millions in seconds. A powerful "homo-sapiens" who believes that a human fetus is just a blob of flesh and that the ill and the old are just dispensable skin and bones can decree the death of millions with a single scrawl on a piece of paper.

At a time when human knowledge doubles every few months, as statisticians are now telling us, and is now reaching the barriers of the miraculous in every field, we can no longer abide living in the darkness with which the mystery of human existence has enveloped humanity throughout the ages. Not when morals, now situational, have not kept up with the technical progress, and for as long as evil is present in the reality of things. For despite our increase in knowledge, our age has become and age of amorality and meaninglessness - the cruelest duo of all precursors of death, and to whom science has given today the ability of destroying us all, incrementally or with a single blast. Today, more than ever before, the very existence of people, nations, and human civilization itself depend on unequivocal answers about the miracle of life, answers leading to a magnanimous and life-loving and eternal-life-giving Creator. At this stage of human history and technical know-how it is madness to continue formulating cultures and forms of government having for basis an unproven theory on life's origin. Naturalism has already cost too many lives since Darwin - multimillions of them.

For many years, because of leaders such as Adams, Washington, Lincoln and others, believers in a God of Creation, we didn't have to worry much about defining life for ourselves. We were protected from the danger of an overpowering government making our life difficult or subjected to man-made threats. America's Founders had seen to it that a well-balanced governing power made no room for the growth of an un-American irreligious elite governing us and being led by *"avarice, ambition, revenge or gallantry"*, as expressed by the second American President, undeterred by people-loving spirituality. The moral values resulting from the Nation's Fathers having properly dignified human life in acknowledging its divine origin protected us and enriched the ethos of America. This privileged people with the honor and moral means of governing themselves, a form of government once sacred to the nation. George Washington knew that well. The first American President, when offered the kingship over the Nation whose independence he had just led in securing, could promptly answer, in leaving the Presidency, *"no, thank you. I am going back to my farm."*

History has now come to a point where we can no longer evade our little Susie's questions. Our God-fearing Fathers are no longer here to define human life for us as being created by God and to guide our government according to life's true meaning and worth. Their writings acknowledging God as the Creator of life are practically neglected, or deemed "unprogressive" or "unscientific". Our present leaders and thinkers are leading us by the wrong answers to those vital questions. We must learn for ourselves the unequivocally correct answers to the questions about the miracle of life and its true origin, worth, meaning, and purpose.

Countries discrediting the God of Creation have gone morally and economically bankrupt before, after their secularly printed political currency is used up by people in their vain quest to purchase meaning and gratification in their dispiriting life. The birthing papers of America, with their emphasis on a Creator God, were designed to make our Nation escape that fate. For many years Americans profited both spiritually and materially from the values absorbed from truths learned from the Judeo/Christian Scriptures, until secular humanism enveloped our culture with self-manufactured ones. To abandon our historical founding documents which spell out the truths about God and human life which are at the heart of that exceptionalism is to place ourselves on the road to spiritual and material bankruptcy.

It was as a believer in a God of Creation that I came across the secret behind America's uniqueness as a Nation that elevated her to greatness. The biblical truth about Creation and the distinctive way in which humanity was created provided me with the answers to my double puzzle - about America and about the meaning of life, with all that this means for us as individuals and as a nation. After living for so long without having solved for myself the puzzle of life and for years living my own life erratically and, like America today, in peril because of it, I suddenly found the right answers, a discovery I actually made during a very human experience.

I made that discovery after being immersed in the vital contents of the same Judeo/Christian Scriptures that inspired the conception of America. I found what I had just learned about human life all there. By paralleling what I had learned about human life with the lives of the Pilgrims and Founders, especially their faith and their responses to the circumstances and the events which our nation's early history relates to us, I realized that they already knew what I had just discovered - that knowledge of theirs, and now, mine, in all its fortuitous details, is what they applied in conceiving America. Thus, unexpectedly, I discovered that the answer to the puzzle of life and the puzzle of America are one and the same.

In the next few Chapters I shall describe the specifics of both discoveries. In dealing with them separately, I expect to disclose the commonality of the two puzzles that taunted me for years, and which, unknown to me, called for the same answer.

Before I identify that final piece of the Puzzle That Is America which I discovered, I must share with the reader the personal experience which prepared me to find what I had been seeking for for so long. This was the incident which gave me as clear an understanding of what life is all about as a human mind - at least, my human mind - can absorb. It also gave me the title for this book.

NINE

A DIFFERENT LOVE SCENE

"Before I formed thee in the belly I knew thee; and before thou camest forth out of the womb I sanctified thee..." (God)

"For a thousand years in thy sight are but as yesterday when it is past, and as a watch in the night." (The Psalms)

It happened on a mild Sunday afternoon.

Empty-nested for a long time, Olivia and I had been experiencing more than ever the closeness to each other which today's style and pace of life so often defraud people of. That fall afternoon, dinner over, Olivia and I found ourselves comfortably seated on our living room couch. In our many years of life together, we have often savored such moments of tenderness and warmth toward each other calling for expression. The impulse comes to us even during activities and often when not alone. With age and more seclusion, these moments have increased in frequency, especially in moments of quietness and stillness. Being by ourselves, we are freer to express that innate human emotion which we have to hold back in the presence of others.

Sometimes we forget that we are not by ourselves. There is a forty-year-old memory which often comes to my mind when I hug my wife. The scene is from Israel, where we were visiting with friends, staff members of a hospital in Nazareth. While waiting for them, we were standing in a crowded hall, surrounded by black-shrouded, self-effacing Moslem women. I was looking at Olivia and, apparently moved by the contrasting ambiance, a love-generated nudge made me fold my arms around her. That was a serious breach of Middle-Eastern decorum! I soon realized my blunder when seeing the poor women scurrying away from us, whom they sadly perceived as engaging in lustful behavior. Olivia and I found ourselves alone in the hall, regretting my gaffe.

That Sunday afternoon at home, we were experiencing one of those tender moments. But its memory of quietness and enchantment produced no regret with it. It was a milestone in my life. It has stayed with me in enduring vividness and joy ever since it happened. What I ended up learning at that time still animates my thoughts, impregnating them with ancillary truths whose vital existence I only conjectured before. What was shown to me then is the essence of what philosophers, poets, and theologians strive to articulate about life. I apprehended those things without having in my mind a previously acquired point of reference which one needs in order to assimilate something new. That justifies my calling it a revelation - that which was given to me unexpectedly, in a moment of time.

I am not surprised that such a guileless display of love toward my sweet wife became God's channel of revelation-giving to this hearty lover. I am more assured than ever that God is, indeed, love. Because of that experience, I now see the relationship between a man and a woman in a more revealing light than I did before. I am more certain now why our Creator has chosen to honor the singular relationship of marriage by making us His partners in the further creation of life.

What happened to me that unforgettable afternoon while sitting with my wife on our living room couch was a very candid, human experience. It was very terrestrial and, at the same time, perhaps, celestial. While my arms were encircling my wife, I was suddenly filled with an intense joy, followed by a heightened sense of happiness. More than ever before, I was enthralled by the synergistic mystery of two souls becoming one, like two hands folded together in prayer.

Times of intense joyfulness like this were not new to me. I was used to experiencing them often. What was different with that particular moment of tenderness was the menacing thought that suddenly surged into my mind in the wake of my sheer joy. The thought came dressed in the dark clothes of finality, of death. It asserted to me, in apparent triumph, the incompatibility of joy and evil. It intimated the baneful ending of all things. It used threatening words like *Death, End, Time, Human Suffering,* and the reluctant altruism of such times implicit in the word *Others.* This funereal thought was never so persuasive, never so credible. I had before detected that same unwelcome thought in moments like these, but the reality of its pronouncement never fully registered on my mind until then. This time, the thought made itself more substantial, and more grim in effectively challenging the existence and indissolubility of such a thing as pure love and joy. It came with a renewed, stronger emphasis on the stark reality of joy-effacing, ever-present evils so active in our world and even within our own hearts.

This time I found myself succumbing to the alarming announcement, and a heart-rending sadness took over the empty space in me which joy suddenly vacated completely, discredited now by the abrupt suggestion of finality and the charge of egotism. I seemed to hear joy cruelly mocking me while departing. "Fool!" it seemed to be shouting at me, "there is an end to all things. The more you love, the more you have to lose when everything ends. Perfect love lost is complete, utter loss. Your love and joy are but runaway stealers of time, irrevocably condemned to die in the gallows of reality!" These and other threats it kept screaming at me like the tragedian it seemed to be portraying.

Next came logic, which mercilessly twisted the dagger it had been just lunged into my chest. It forced me to determine for myself which was the more wicked source of my utter sadness now. Was it the present, acute intellectual awareness of the inexorable reality of the unstoppable demise of personal joy through death, at any time? Or was it the realization that joy and love had been insensitively misrepresenting their integrity all through the years? Or was it the sudden realization that joy and love had been clothing the nakedness of their finality and self-seeking with costumes of endlessness and selflessness? I could have easily discovered the sham at any time, and yet, enthralled and acquiescent, I had allowed it to freely play-act before me all my life. Contrary to its former inebriating claims, I was now suddenly discovering, and now agonizingly believing, that throughout my happy married life, joy had always retained the right, with cold unconcern, to schedule itself to fade into nothingness at any time it pleased.

A blasphemous conclusion followed the quick succession of joy and sadness: the Eternal Love-Giver has to be, then, a reneging debtor to humanity, despite His heavenly wealth and our earthly poverty. Considering the value of what will be taken away from me, He must be more of a taker than a giver, a mocker of our humanity. This logical conclusion frightened me for a moment. "This is the place where a man can find himself cursing God", I thought to myself, "or discovering that He has never been there after all". These last thoughts brought me, swiftly, to a deep conviction that I had trespassed on God's private territory of reality. This calming realization made me see myself as a rebellious holder of a self-righteous indignation, a wimpy accuser of the guiltless Creator of such wondrous things as love and joy. It was only by God's grace, I know now, but I responded to my intellectual tantrum with voluntary, repentant humility. I found myself reacting as Job did in his misery, *"Though He* [God] *slay me, yet will I trust in him..."*. Fully conscious of this sin, I acknowledged my dark, heretical flow of logic.

It was at that precise moment that true light burst into the abyss where I found myself. It came from a point *outside* my mental canvas - the only place, I later learned, from which the authentic picture of human life can be glimpsed. It absorbed with its brilliancy the pulses of my mind without annulling my thoughts. A lucid, wordless perception, it revealed to my mind's eyes every glorious and permanent feature of redeemed life, with all its attendant joys which are indeed capable of dissolving time and superseding all sorrows, all self-centeredness - a life only Absolute Love and Omnipotence could have created. The picture of life I saw at that moment was extraordinarily limpid, as pristine as the angels must have first beheld human life in the Garden of Eden at the moment of its creation, before the Fall.

It took every ounce of my mental power to behold life's holy sight. I was now possessed by an overwhelming certainty that human life, with its originally programmed love and joy, besides being precious beyond reckoning, is unending, no matter how evil and death depict it now. That as darkness gives light its very existence and meaning, nothing is more capable of defining life than death. That the gift of life flows into eternity, since it is impossible for God to be a recalcitrant, mocking giver. That even what it has of good in time is a harbinger of the eternal best yet to come. That He who created us in His own image and likeness planted His human creation in His own bed of eternity. That life comes with seeds of eternal joy and love already sown in the soil of its ever-living soul, whatever the condition may be of the human garden plot - ready to blossom in any season or weather. That human life is so much more than the time-restricted output of vital organs that have not yet ceased to function, and much more than one's sustained breath. That life exists in its own right, gloriously independent of perishable physical organs or the psychological features we try to build selfhood with, and it is designed to carry our own, personal identity forever. That conceived by the same divine love that makes One the three Persons of the Trinity, human life is the brightest, most wonderful of all creation among all the wonders teeming in the vastness of the created universe.

That there are as many eternal sources of fulfillment prepared for human life as there are planets and stars which no man or computer can number, in a world created for humanity's and its Creator's pleasure. That suffused by God's own breath at creation and again at recreation through Redemption, life is a holy thing in itself, despite sins. That evils within and without people which obscure its glow are but passing clouds in a world still being guided to a final redemption already primed and graciously presented to the individual's choice of joining in or abstaining from. That death, which we erroneously think of as the opposite of life, is just the black cloth that jewelers use as background to show forth a gem's luminosity, its mesh of evil and suffering being but the threads of the weaving. That divinely created and then rebirthed life is designed to be eternally throbbing with the unending joys which are its ever healthy, living cells, for eternity has no measurable length, and time is but a dot in an ever expanding, boundless universe. That in God's vision for His creation, life is to have a thrilling purpose for now and for eternity - far beyond human ability to fully comprehend as yet, though just a glimpse of it now is enough to make us realize the immense richness of such a gift and then go on to live and love accordingly, sustained and inspired by that very richness.

In that fortuitous moment while hugging my wife, I discovered the key designed to secure the means to live undisturbed and unshaken by the present mysteries of life with all its complexities and paradoxes of pleasure and pain, faith and doubt, bliss and tragedy. And the key is this: while still in our earthly waiting-room of eternity, we must learn to extend our mental lines of understanding from every one of life's facets, whether clear or enigmatic, to the point of infinity which is outside the picture's frame. For that is where God's home is as the Uncreated Creator of *everything that is* - the all-knowing, love-driven and final Arranger of every human circumstance designed to lead His human creation to a restoring experience of personal redemption. For "... *all things work together for good to them that love God, to them who are the called according to His purpose."*

God's own eternity and ours form together the measuring rod of grandeur, the defining words for understanding life's mysteries; the source of explanation and remedy for all our confusion and emotional illnesses, for the Lord is the truthful Revealer of meaning and purpose, the consummate Aesthetician and Restorer of our faded portraits of life. Nothing mysterious in life can be really threatening when viewed through its Creator's lens of eternal, absolute wisdom, righteousness, and all-redeeming love. To take our eyes off that infinity is to incapacitate ourselves to live a meaningful life. It is to open the gates of our life to an odious parade of sure-conquering evils and doubts, even those deceitfully arrayed in costumes of good.

But even after being given so magnificent a view of human life's true picture as conceived for eternity and all that that means, I was still temporarily troubled by a lingering uneasiness. I was questioning in my mind how we, as earthlings still, can maintain all those lines to infinity unbroken when there is yet a sure physical death ahead to be experienced. My questioning derived from more than a justifiable abhorrence and natural fear of death. I was still seeing death, unpredictable and yet inevitable, as perfectly capable of cutting off, on her own, our lines of infinity-thinking, even if just for a disconcerting second. Wouldn't that disrupt the flow of eternity as it did before, when it first broke into the reality of things with Adam's fall to construct here our prison of time? Suddenly, it became crucially important to me to know, while still living in the convoluted now, how the two ends of *before* and *after* the human heart's last beat could life be mended together whole. To accord with the wholeness of life as just revealed to me, the mending had to be so perfect as to be imperceptible. It had to have no seams, no blemishing scar, as if a disruption had never occurred. I was arguing that death had already once interrupted our Creator's eternal plan for the life He created. I still saw even the simple anticipation of unavoidable death tarnishing my earthly joys. I was seeing in the wake of my questioning an unexpected shadow starting to spread itself over the glorious picture of life which I still beheld.

A surprising answer, cautiously taking another chance on the smallness of my faith, satisfied my last query and sealed forever the revelation of life's authenticity given to me on that unforgettable Sunday afternoon. Again, by God's grace, my little faith still held firm after hearing the answer which was to banish all doubts and give full credence to the eternal, immaculate beauty of the picture of life which I beheld. I heard no voice, just the whisper of Reason providing the answer to be added to the picture of life still before me. I read the answer's wording as if it were digitally appended to the picture of life still before me. I had often heard and read those words before, but for the first time I understood the full depth of their meaning and how this can quell the anxiety which our inborn thirst for wholeness brings. The words are from the Bible: *"...whosoever liveth and believeth in me shall never die."*

For the first time I knew that, somehow, these words from the very lips of the Incarnate God's said to a grieving girl whose brother had, ironically, just died, and whom He was about to raise from the dead, were not hyperbolical. I knew then that they express a vital truth in a dimension of its own, a truth intrinsically capable of causing human beings to actually experience deathless life while in time and space. The Pilgrims did, key America's fathers did, George Washington did, and because they did they were made ready *"to assume among the Powers of the Earth, the separate and equal Station to which the Laws of Nature and of Nature's God entitle them"* - and a new Nation was born to live under the Creator of Life Who has *"conquered death"*. Since then, countless others have experienced the comforting truth of human eternality. Lincoln did, many other leaders of our Nation did, Olivia, my dear American wife did - and for that, they never changed except when growing further in all that is good. Now, lastly, this small lump from the huddled masses did, too.

My Puzzle That Is America was about to be solved. I found The Puzzle of Life turning out to be but the actual picture-guide of America herself, directing me to the correct pieces by which my Puzzle of America was to be solved. I didn't see this picture-guide until that mild Sunday afternoon when Eternal Love became for me another synonym for Life. I was ready then, and we are ready now, to place the last puzzle piece where it belongs.

TEN

THE BOOK OF LIFE
IN PICTURES

*"Eye hath not seen, nor ear heard, neither have entered
into the heart of man, the things which God hath prepared
for them that love Him".* (St. Paul, quoting the Prophet Isaiah)

While organizing my thoughts with a view to how best articulate further what I learned about human life as seen through its Creator's eyes, I read the first chapter of a book by Christian apologist Ravi Zacharias. The book, titled *The Grand Weaver*, was not published yet at the time of this writing. I read that chapter in the latest triannual communiqué called "Just Thinking", which the Author's organization mails out. In the book, God is pictured as a loving, all-knowing weaver for whom all the characteristics and circumstances of any particular individual's life make up the strands. Its message is about how those characteristics and circumstances, no matter how ugly or undesirable they seem to sight, perception, or feeling, have been especially designed by The Grand Weaver with His eternal and joyful purposes for that particular person in view. Those strands are precisely the ones He Himself chose in order to create the unique pattern of beauty He envisioned for the eternal life of each person He brings into being.

I was about to start this chapter of my book with the words, "God, Who never misses and shall never miss a shot..." when I read Dr. Zacharias' masterfully written piece. The article made me realize how plebeian my metaphor sounded next to the one devised by that scholar. While reading that chapter of his coming book I realized that the Author was painting life using the same model I had used and whose features I tried so hard to depict. But he does it so much better than I that I had to borrow the picture from his easel. I feel I can only do justice to the writer by quoting parts of the chapter verbatim, hoping that Zondervan, the publisher of *"The Grand Weaver"*, will allow me to do that.

The writer was telling his readers about listening to a lecture at John Hopkins University given by Dr. Francis Collins, of human DNA mapping fame and a Christian scientist. The talk was to be followed by Ravi Zacharias' own address on the theme "What Does it Mean to be Human". Here is part of what the apologist wrote about that experience: In his last slide, he [Dr. Collins] showed two pictures side by side. On the left appeared a magnificent photo of the stained-glass rose window from Yorkminster Cathedral in Yorkshire, England, its symmetry radiating from the center, its colors and geometric patterns spectacular - clearly a work of art purposefully designed by a gifted artist. Its sheer beauty stirred the mind. On the right side of the screen appeared a slide showing a cross section of a strand of human DNA. The picture did more than take away one's breath; it was awesome in the profoundest sense of the term - not just beautiful, but overwhelming. And it almost mirrored the pattern of the rose window in Yorkminster. The intricacy of the DNA's design that pointed to the Transcendent One astonished those who are themselves the design and who have been created semi-transcendent by design. We see ourselves only partially, but through our Creator's eyes, we see our transcendence. In looking at our DNA, the subject and the object came together. The audience gasped at the sight, for it saw itself. The design, the color, the splendor of the design left everyone speechless, even though it is this very design that makes us capable of speech. Because of this design, we can think in profound ways, but felt paralyzed by the thought and could go no further. Because of that design we were capable of love and suddenly could see the loveliness of who we are.

Yet, it was only the present, frail human body, marred by the Original Sin and destined to be returned to the earth from where it came, whose beauty of composition Dr. Zacharias so vividly describes. There is astonishing beauty still in the temporary residence of the eternal soul, the "body of humiliation" as the Apostle Paul calls our bodies in his letter to the Philippians. Today, millennia after creation, modern Science is finally capable of seeing some of what God saw, and understanding why He responded the way He did while beholding the first man whom He had just fashioned. The book of Genesis records our Creator's reaction after creating Adam by quoting God's Own words, *"It is very good!"* as He admired the masterpiece of complexity and beauty He had just created. After the fall of the first couple, the Lord seemed to have been reluctant to allow the penal consequence of sin - bodily death - to be carried out. I fancy this to be the reason why people lived for many hundreds of years at the dawn of human history, though sin had already introduced into all matter an obsolescence which was not originally built into it by our Creator. It was as if God loathed the idea of having the beauty of His once eternal and wholesome creation, bearing His Own image and likeness, to be defaced by old age and death.

Ravi Zachariah then goes on to tell his experience of seeing his father-in-law, a dignified man in his eighties, having to suffer the indignities a dying person often goes through while waiting for death to come. At the end of the chapter, the author contrasts that unpleasantness with a moving testimony to the ultimate in dignifying splendor and beauty awaiting the redeemed ones as the continuance of our earthly life: "As strength was leaving his body and he could no longer communicate with loved ones", he writes, "he suddenly opened his eyes and said twice, quietly and clearly, 'Amazing! It's just amazing!' A few hours later, he again stirred, reached out his thin arms to his wife of sixty-two years, and said, 'I love you!' Then he let his head drop back on his pillow. Those were his last words. Within twenty-four hours he was gone. That was the end. Or was it the beginning? When you know the Grand Weaver, it is neither. It was a punctuation mark in the design that he was about to see and enjoy forever."

What Dr. Zachariah's relative experienced when leaving time and entering eternity was a sampling of the first sights and sounds of eyes and ears belonging to a new mode of existence. He was probably having a preview of the *"things"* that God has *"prepared"* for those who love Him which can't yet *"enter"* the human mind - the utmost good and beauty his soul was created for - the good and beauty that even unbelievers seek on earth while foolishly shunning their true source, good and beauty which only an all-powerful and loving Creator can design and offer. He was having a foretaste of the promised New Earth and New Heaven where the redeemed soul's amplified senses perceive pure beauty in depth and substance. He was realizing that he was being freed to finally reach the infinitude for which we were created and which we can on earth only guess at and yearn for - the believer's total freedom as expressed by the Prophet Isaiah when he wrote, *"But they that wait upon the Lord shall renew their strength; they shall mount up with wings as eagles: they shall run, and not be weary; and they shall walk, and not faint"*. And he was probably hearing the *"unspeakable words, which is not lawful for man to utter"* of St. Paul's death-foiling vision of Heaven, and translating them with lips not yet free from human limitations with his non-descriptive *"Amazing! It is just amazing"*. Ravi Zachariah's relative's soul - the real person - was starting to ascend to the skies with *"the greatest of ease"*, with no need of balloons or bird-like wings, the starting-out point of glorious living in a place where *"death is no more"*; a place where one *"could have danced all night and still have danced some more"*, then *"spread"* the *"wings"* and do *"a thousand things"* which couldn't be *"done before"*; a realm of complete freedom from earthly bonds which the atheist author of *Pygmalion* could only use as a figure of speech; a realm where *"the inside"* was *"greater than the outside"* of C.S. Lewis's Narnian world.

One of the greatest divine temporary palliatives for human suffering is to know for sure beforehand, and by God's mercy, that the very moment believers stop breathing is when they start to really live. This knowledge, this certainty, not only gives us a reason to live our earthly life with gusto for the joy of anticipation of the utmost of all good things, but it frees us from the fear of death which is in reality but a phantom. Living every day in this faith, we can wait with patience and awe for our Creator and Redeemer to call us back to Himself when we are made ready. What Dr. Zachariah and I describe here is not fiction, intellectual play, or self-induced dreaming. What we write about is duly expressed in the Holy Scriptures and historically certified by the actual experience of millions of redeemed souls who, like Ravi's father-in-law, had suddenly been given *"eyes to see and ears to hear"*. We are calling attention to an existing reality waiting for all those who in this world *"live by faith and not by sight,"* in the words of the Apostle Paul - a man who actually saw with his own eyes, not just with the eyes of faith, the wonders of a heavenly reality which naturalists, in their proud negation of a Creator God, miss entirely.

What makes the reading of Dr. Zachariah's story even more heartening is to know that the human experience he relates is not unique. There have been thousands of others who, *"who are saved"* as the Holy Scriptures refers to individuals embracing redemption, have been made able to see and revel in that marvelous picture of sinless reality at an otherwise frightening moment. Their fainting human eyes were made capable of beholding the wonderful sights and truths which God has designed for us, normally seen only by spiritual bodies. Countless believers have had such experiences since our Savior's historical resurrection - a phenomenon which speaks of the existence of another dimension in Creation which secular humanism denies. Tragically, the opposite is also true. Stalin's daughter's description of her father's dying moment has a poignancy unmatched by any written human drama: she tells how the unrepentant murderer of millions died shaking his fist at heaven. One is left to wonder whom or what the Russian tyrant was throwing his last bit of wrath to, while Ravi's father-in-law died with the word *love* on his lips.

I take the "punctuation mark" of our Christian apologist as the "seamless mending" I sought during my vision of human life as originally designed and as recreated in redemption. My next job is to tell how this can be so and still keep demanding thinkers happy. There is a reasonable explanation for the phenomenon of punctuation marks and seamlessness between time and eternity, earth and Heaven. Jesus used many striking hyperboles when trying to make us understand the deep things of God. But when He told Martha that those who believe in Him shall never die, He was not using a figure of speech. This truth nobody can afford to be unaware of, specially in these days when the last chapter of history seems to be in the process of being written.

ETERNALITY

No, I don't mind being so old.
I'll tell you why:
You see those marvelous tints of gold
In the azure sky?
You don't? Right there! Above the blues
Of towering mountains
Where flow the clear, celestial hues
Of living fountains!

Oh! I don't mind my poor eyesight
Down here. No! Never!
Not when my faith sees now a sight
I'll see forever!

Come further up. I want you here
On higher ground
To hear the music. Can't you hear
This heavenly sound?
Oh! I don't mind not hearing well
Down here. No! Never!
For I shall hear this glorious swell
Of songs forever!

Weak heart, you say? That's where I'm made
A New Creation!
My Savior wrote here my new name
And destination!

Oh! I don't mind life growing dim,
No! Never! Never!
Not when I know I'll be with Him
And live forever.

ELEVEN

NO WALLS

Verily, verily, I say unto you, If a man keep my saying, he shall never see death. (Jesus)

The meaning of life is that it stops (Novelist Franz Kafka)

There is an old cemetery in South Canaan, a quiet hamlet in Northeast Pennsylvania near the little town of Lake Ariel, where we live. We have our family burial plot there. The secluded community cemetery has a lake nearby and is surrounded by old stone walls and luxuriant trees. Its scenery is a lovely natural chronometer keeping pace with the seasons following one another with their telltale colors and weather's changing patterns. On Veteran's Days we watch in silent veneration as the breeze gently waves little American flags over the graves of patriots who served the Nation, some of them paying the price of patriotism with their very lives. Multinational family names of dead and living people are engraved on weathered or recently erected tombstones. The engravings are like calling cards identifying America as the world's place of refuge, a haven for seekers of life's earthly fulfillment. It is the perfect spot for another Brown - Olivia - who, for love, became a de Carvalho, to have her body laid to rest some day next to the foreigner who completed her love by reciprocating it wholeheartedly.

When Olivia's parents died, she had a stone bench placed right between the two sets of graves. It separates the ones where

"Pa's" and "Ma Brown's" bodies wait for the Resurrection Day and the sites prepared for the two de Carvalhos who are to follow them some day. There is no tombstone there for any of us, as customarily erected. We have an engraving cut on top of the bench with the summations of our four earthly lives written with an economy of words. There, my wife and I often sit and pray. There, a contentment springing from a source we know to come from another world discourages passing sadness and fears, and dries up misleading tears. We never think of our dead ones as absentees. Ours and the Browns' lives seem even more real and eternal to us when surrounded by death-reminding tombs.

To live daily with the awareness of this most real of life's events while seemingly not caring to have to face it can be perceived as the most self-injurious form of carelessness. Our apparent coziness with what is called humanity's worse enemy is not a result of that shortcoming, or a product of morbidity or flippancy. Olivia and I are not naive, either. We have visited many, many countries and walked on many paths unknown to indulged tourists. We have witnessed human lives being lived under irreversibly tragic conditions where death is a constant threat. We have been acquainted with human suffering and the ugly realities of life and death at their darkest. We have often met evil and hopelessness face to face. We have seen death aiming at us from the barrel of a cocked gun in the hand of a desperado. We have been on high seas as fifty-foot waves threatened for days on end to swallow our old ship at any moment.

All of us live every day with death constantly at our heels. We even forget, foolishly so, that it is there. Yet, we know that it can overtake us at any time of day or night, often dispensing with warnings. We are all unavoidably liable to be diagnosed at any time with the illness that will sooner or later take our bodies to our graves. There is always the ever present possibility of the telephone ringing at any time with a weeping caller at the other end telling us of a dear one whose soul just left this world. We know that death, with all the pains that often precede and follow it, is real. Only fools deny this ever-present player in the drama of reality.

At the same time, we believe in the Incarnate Savior, and in the truth of His words that those who believe in Him shall never die, with the same certainty that we are still alive and standing on terra firma. How can we take as factual our Redeemer's promise that we shall never die? Are we two of those people who have been conditioned to deceive themselves with religious illusions and false hope, as atheists and skeptics think of those who believe in an incarnate, life-redeeming, and resurrected Creator God? Is it possible that there is a provision, a phenomenon which is so real as to obliterate from our consciousness the dark reality of death, thus giving credence to the literalness of the Creator's words without harming reason? Is our Savior speaking of an existing divine antidote to the reality of human death, or are they but a rhetorical placebo to sooth the fear of dying? Who is telling the truth, the Incarnate God and Life Creator, or Franz Kafka?

We are not alone in taking those divine words literally. Across from where Olivia and I meditate while seated on our tomb-bench is another cemetery. It lies next to St. Tikhon's Orthodox Seminary and Monastery. In this religious community, the statement of the One whose death was designed to bring forth life is not taken as paradoxical or metaphorical either. The Savior's pledge that those who believe in Him shall never die has been for centuries at the center of the Orthodox Church's form of worship. Assertively, the shape of the ceiling and the painting of their temple' interior are drawn to represent Heaven. The decor of the place where seminarians, professors, and monks worship responds affirmatively to our Redeemer's pledge of no-death to believers. While people worship, everything around and about them combines to open their every sense to envision the unseen believers of years past present with them in the building. Their ancient way of acknowledging the truth of the

Savior's promise is significant. By worshipping the way they do, the ancient Orthodox Church pragmatically affirms life while celebrating death's vanquishment. Those believers of the past are perceived as invisible only to the limited sight of earthlings. Visible worshippers commune with the invisible, but also real, ones. There is no wall between them. On Easter Sunday we can hear the joyful voices of living believers singing along with the ringing of bells the greatest news ever to come to mortal ears: "Christ is risen from the dead, trampling down death by death, and upon those in the tombs bestowing life!" You can almost hear Nature echoing back the eternal refrain, "Halleluiah! Halleluiah! Halleluiah!"

Have these people been deceiving themselves for nearly two thousand years? Common sense alone tells us that that cannot be. Self-deception of that sort cannot last for long past humanity's ever growing sophistication. Realizing that our Creator deals with life and death as the two sides of the same coin when purchasing our redemption, Christian orthodoxy deals with life and death in the same tone of voice. The believer knows that it is the death of a resurrected Incarnate Creator that produces the life which is His very life. *"He will swallow up death in victory; And the Lord God will wipe away tears from off all faces"*, Isaiah wrote when prophesying about this after-effect of the incarnation, death, and resurrection of life's Creator. That prophet's body of predictions about these cosmic events was historically fulfilled in minute detail, and so did his prophecy about the eradication of death. Six centuries later, just before His painful death and glorious resurrection, the Incarnate God informed humanity through His Apostles then still in the making, *"Because I live, ye shall live also"*. And that this life is sinless and eternal is contextually implicit.

Franz Kafka is also quoted as saying that "anyone who keeps the ability to see beauty never grows old". It seems the writer was seeing something about life worth seeing - something usually expressed only by those to whom what is good in life surpasses what is bad in their perception and personal experience. That writer ignored at that point the black background already on the canvas where he was painting life even while interpreting death as final. One wonders what he did with the inescapable realization that a time-limited, earthly definition of life is not enough to provide it with fullness of meaning. There are millions of people in our sin-torn world who, in their suffering, would resent Kafka's veiled and, to many unbelievers' view, unwarranted existential positivism. The writer might as well have joined the poet compatriot of mine who ended a sonnet on life with that resigning lamentation, "Madman, no one can define life. Just limit yourself to living". The Gospel truth is that nothing defines life better than vanquished death.

Franz Kafka, like most of us before being able to see life as originally created and then recreated through Redemption, was not able to see the forest for the trees. I have experienced this misreading myself. I spent the first years of my life counting on my penchant to see beauty, coupled with discounting suffering while closing my eyes to the reality of physical death, as a recipe for satisfying living. I only realized how soul-debilitating this diet is when having dinner with a famous writer in an equally famous Manhattan restaurant, a celebrity who wanted to introduce me to his literary world. A biblical expression long buried in my mind came suddenly to light for me when I heard this great litterateur shouting gutter obscenities to a waiter he was upset with - *"The beauty of holiness"*, a devotional expression used by a prophet and a poet whose books are included in the canon of the Holy Scriptures. Beauty, holiness, and eternality are the true features of the life that believers can be endowed to live, from the moment they believe to the end of their allotted earthly time, and on into eternity. The uncreated light of eternity can pass through the wall of time, lending meaning to human life and causing us to live more abundantly, as promised by the Creator of Life.

RESURRECTION BELLS

In priestly garments, Aaron ventures through the veil
Bearing on onyx stones Jehovah's children's names.
Will God's wrath fall this time? Will Mercy again prevail?
Can blood of lambs still satisfy His Justice's claims?

In silent fear, the people strain their ears to hear
Coming from bells tied to Aaron's skirts the sound that tells
Of fatal verdict held in check another year.
That's all they hoped to learn from yet unsilenced bells.

Then, Mercy and Justice found in Love a holy tryst.
There, all our sins were placed within Christ's guiltless breast.
The Saving Wrath was spent there.
Slain was God's Lamb-Priest
And the awesome ring of man-made bells was put to rest.

New sounds surround priestly robes lasting now forever.
Bells of redemption toll in joyful, ceaseless ring!
Three days - that's all the time it took for God to sever
Our ties to death, its fears, finality and sting!

TWELVE

A NATION UNDER GOD

"Blessed is the Nation, whose God is the Lord". (The Psalms)

"...*Laws of Nature and of Nature's God*" - You can seldom read words with that much depth and range of meaning as these words so felicitously put together in a phrase, except when studying the Judeo/Christian Holy Scriptures with their wealth of vital and reliable information about humanity, the world, and God. In these seven words which America's Fathers inserted in the first paragraph of our Declaration of Independence, there is utilitarian theology without the suggestion of religious abstractions, plus science without scientific terminology. It is just plain, recognizable reality. Contrary to what our present culture insinuates, science and the Bible never clash against each other, and they never will, except in our sectarian, compartmentalizing minds. These words speak of an intelligent, wise way of acknowledging God and Him as Creator of the world in claiming people's right and privilege, as His creatures, to have a Nation Under God if they so choose - all this without being just "religious".

With these words so ingeniously put together, our Nation's Founders were able to connect the idea of what they called *"True Religion"*, to Nature and on to the Creator of Reality, not just to dogmatic concepts - and the unbreakable threefold cord, whether holding the weight of humanity or the new Nation was securely tied to God.

America's historical exceptionalism began with this masterful piece of clear thinking and meticulous writing in the Nation's birthing document which portrays her very soul and boldly imprints her identity on the pages of history. And our Founders meant their every word or they wouldn't have pledged, as they did, their *"life and fortune and sacred honor"* in their faith in God on behalf of the new nation as the circumstances of history demanded of them. And for the sake of the new nation, some of them did lose both life and fortune for their honesty and bravery, while keeping their sacred honor.

Their words, which narrate the event of America's beginning, echo those in the Bible's book of Genesis which describes the beginning of the world and life. The Founders' Bible is the same Judeo/Christian Scriptures which provided the basis for Western Culture, the Book that not only covers human history but also its consummation; the Book that has humanity and our relationship to our Creator, to Reality, to Nature, and to one another as its main theme. There is as much depth and range of meaning in the detailed biblical account of Creation as there is in the America's Fathers' brilliant introductory words of our Nation's birth certificate. The biblical author of Genesis also uses precise wording in reporting the cosmic events of Creation. The two sets of choice words, that of Moses and that of the Fathers of America, link together the genesis of our Nation and the genesis of humanity, world, and reality. In this, the true meaning of human life as first originated, and the true identity of America as first conceived, explain each other. Therein lies the secret of America's exceptionalism, which has led her to greatness. Therein lies the final clue for the completion to my Puzzle That Is America and Puzzle That Is Life, neatly exposing itself to the careful reader between the two wording documenting two births - the birth of Human Beings and the birth of a Nation. The reader will discover this last piece, unexpectedly to me, a single one, but designed to fit both puzzles, before this chapter is over.

Though all of the marvels of Creation is still unfathomable to human minds, the Bible reports to us some stunning, meaningful details of how it was done by having us think of God, Who is Himself still beyond the range of our sensory organs, as if possessing the bodily features of His creatures. Theologians call this *anthropomorphism* - a verbal and gestural means we connect with our bodies by which God's infinite mind is enabled to communicate with finite ones. This makes it possible for both ancient and modern minds to have a modicum of needed understanding of God and His activities. It makes it possible for us to grasp the import of Creation for the lives of people and the life of nations.

We read in the Judeo/Christian Scripture's book of Genesis that things and animals owe their existence to God's *spoken* words: (This reminds us moderns of our voice-activated electronic gadgets that print or do what the speaker says or commands. Just while I was typing these words we got a call from Susie, our daughter, hundreds of miles away. She was driving her new car with the latest in human communication - she had just said, "Call Mother", and seconds later our telephone rang without her having to dial the number)*"And God said, Let be light: and there was light"*. From the Gospel of John we learn that *"In Him* [the Creator] *was life"*, and *"In the beginning was the Word, and the Word was with God, and the Word was God"*.

With a series of " *let-there-be's"* spoken by God - " *let there be water... vegetation, living creatures..."* things came into existence as commanded by the Uncreated Speaker. But when it came to the creation of human beings we are told that this was accomplished with more than words; for we learn that our Creator formed the original *"Man"* with His Own *"hands"*. This distinction in the mode of Creation of things and "Man" is of extreme importance in understanding human life, and from this understanding, the meaning of it to us and to our Nation. What is also vitally instructive in the Creator's procedures in Creation, especially to freedom-enriched America, is that

Genesis tells us that God *"chose"* to create the human being. God's written words *"... Let Us* **make** *man"* clearly speak of the divine *"will"* of the Triune Being, of His mind having been made up at a certain point in the creative process, about creating *"Man"*. And then, that making was to be done *"in our* [the Trinity's] *image, after our likeness"*, a tri-phased image and likeness as our own science would describes the set of three minimum dimensions we need to perceive anything - height, breath, and width.

Then the Bible specifically cites the next "activity" performed by our Creator to actually bring about the cosmic emergence of living humanity: *"And the Lord God* **formed** *man of the dust of the ground, and* **breathed** *into his nostrils the breath of life"*. This particularity in Creation teaches us that there is both Nature and God's nature in you and me. And the residue of His divinity is still in us after the Fall - a small token of the divine which, though very small indeed, characterizes us as sentient human beings, not merely another animal "species". Even in its smallness, it makes us capable of realizing love in our *hearts* and eternity in our *souls,* with the promised *Spirit* enabling us to return to the original fullness of the divine image and likeness through personal redemption - the regeneration that initiates the return to us of the lost attributes of the Godhead, though remaining forever the created human beings that we are. Some theologians think of this token as the purveyor of our *conscience,* something we are free to ignore if we so choose, since we have a will of our as one of the *likeness* our Creator sculptured in His human creation.

Some of the greatest tragedies in human past and current history come from the failure of religions to recognize human life as being created in God's image and likeness, which is the very foundation of meaning leading to life's worth and purpose. This failure is what causes people of all religionist persuasions, including Christendom, to invent the most painful ways to torture and kill religious adversaries - despite both killers and victims carrying in themselves the image and likeness of their Holy Creator. A side-effect of this barbaric way of continuing the rebellion against God started at the Fall and now, under supposed religious mandate, is the number of skeptics and atheists it encourages. The conceivers and founders of our Nation must have realized this as their lives were threatened by the English State Religion's cruel indifference to the Dissenters' humanity. Wisely, they found a way for the God of Creation to take His primacy in the formation of America by acknowledging Him as Creator, rather than by designing a human path of dogmas to connect God with the nation they created. In terms of national identity, the "laws of Nature and of Nature's God" form the context for the Founders' "True Religion" and the Pilgrims' "Gospel", terms which our Nation's Fathers used in founding papers and historians transcribed in their history books.

There is one more vital truth we can learn from the peculiarity of Creation which lends to America one of her best features - freedom. Freedom-lovers in this Country often speak about our prized truth that human freedom "comes from God, not from the government". This fact alone has what it takes in depth and energy to bring Americans back to the Founders' God, so that we might continue to keep what we have secured spiritually, morally, and economically. But to better appreciate this gift we have from God - freedom - we must attend to how the Holy Scriptures indicates to us that, indeed, our personal freedom is intrinsically connected to God - through His will to which performance we owe our being while discrediting naturalism which deems humans as just another "animal species": When engaged in His activities as Creator, God could as well have said, "Let Us *not* make Man", and we would not exist at all; or, if committed to it for some reason beyond our perception, God could have said "Let us make Man, but *not* in our image and likeness", and naturalism would have been justified in listing us next to "simian species" The word *will* would lose its meaning entirely if these two possibilities were not there. *Will* necessitates freedom to be carried out, or it would be a constant source of frustration in the absence of freedom. That is how we can know and affirm that human freedom comes from God, not from any other source.

The same will that God exercised in Creation has been bequeathed to us as created by Him in his image and likeness. In my mother-tongue, theologians call this divine likeness of ours to that of God, *"livre-arbitreo"*, a phrase signifying the freedom to use your will simply because it exists, even as you exist as a human being. Like breathing, this is a gift we all use, whether conscious of having it or not. This means that *every* human being, whether man or woman, whether black, white, yellow or red, rich or poor, old or young, ugly or handsome, healthy or sickly, still in the womb or breathing on its own - has a right to God-bestowed freedom; this for the simple fact of God's image and likeness is still found in everyone of them.

Obviously, this means also that to do either harm or good to people or to ourselves as we exercise our freedom of will is to do harm or do good to the One Who created people. This must be recognized by all players in humanity's drama of life, something that only America so far seems to have once understood as crucial for peace and prosperity. If human freedom doesn't exist pragmatically, it is foolish to entertain it as existing conceptually. To understand this and behave accordingly is, therefore, vital for humanity's well-being. It has always been so. It must be learned by all humanity that it is indeed so, especially today. Our own civilization will end in the chaos of a prophesied Armageddon if this is overlooked. The harm we can do to one another with today's enormous knowledge and technology, when morals are being dictated by relativism and not issuing from an Absolute and Creator God, can be devasting absolute harm. Only the humbling of our will to accept the divine standard of moral absolutes can bring us salvation - the standard our Founders adopted and set in the foundation of America in acknowledging God, as the *"Supreme Being"* and Creator.

The basis for our founding statesmen's drafting of our Constitution is the same one our Creator used in the drafting of the Ten Commandments. That is why America's legal system was unapologetically based on that summation of Mosaic laws - principles which today our secularists and atheists want our Nation to ignore, this bringing great damage to our society. Because of our bent for sinning, our holy Creator provided us with a pattern for doing good when we direct the will He granted us to do good - just as God is good, and not evil. This divine pattern is vital for America, a Nation of self-governing people as our Founders politically designed our form of government. This Nation cannot subsist without God's pattern. That's certainly what John Adams had in mind when writing that America's Constitution was framed for *"religious"* people only.

Like God's our will is exercised through freedom. Viewed from the angle of human logic, God took an enormous risk when including will and freedom as two of our likenesses to Him. But, again, by the same logic, how could we truly love Him back, He Who is called Love itself, when love requires reciprocation by will, through freedom to be true and complete?

That we have a will of our own is what enhances our worth as much as our responsibility for being human beings. Our *will* can bring out in us all the gentleness of a mother cradling a baby in her arms, or the power behind the complexity of factors of landing a man on the moon, or the acquiring of skill and determination to produce the ultimate weapon for the extermination of human life, or for letting an once romantic marriage end in the coldness of a court of law. More importantly, its conscious use determines whether we'll be living our lives through a path leading us to the glory of our original creation, the ultimate reason for our existence, through repentance and redemption, or to the doom already decreed by the human rebellion against our Creator God. Our will makes us responsible for our own soul's earthly contentment and eternal fulfillment. And, while we are still on earth, our *will* can bring us back to the Pilgrims' and the Founders' America. Or join others in allowing the creation of an America of the secular humanist intended to become just another barrio of the "World Village".

The biblical account of life's origin, clearly expressed in its history of Creation, is at the heart of the vital body of truths upon which our Nation was established. Unlike other nations, America was not crafted by the sword; weapons came later to preserve that which was crafted. The seeds used in the planting of America were Faith in a God Who, in the words of the Bible, created *"all there is"*, including *Man*, soul-bearing creature not accidentally sprouted out of sluggish slime. These healthy seeds took, grew, and became the fruits which invigorated America from birth to maturity. The priceless gifts of human worth and freedom which our founding documents acknowledged and vouchsafed for us by founding our Nation "under God" are directly connected with this knowledge. Together, biblical quotations, letters, sermons, and other writings still extant demonstrate that America's history, when not distorted or misinterpreted by biased revisionists, confirms this truth about her birth, a truth of critical importance for us today.

The mustard-size image and likeness that our Creator left in us is capable, in God's economy of things, to make the soul's worth higher than the mountain our Creator said we can move with a tiny amount of faith; higher, our Lord has told us in His Own words, than the worth of the *"whole world"*. That explains the greatness of America for being born and raised under the God of Creation - a people's faith reaching for that greatness with a very small but powerful remainder of the God of Creation's image, left over from the first rebellion against God as Father. But that faith, if willingly extinguished by us or misplaced by our pride in denying God as Creator, will lower America to the undistinguishing common denominator of nations lying in the valleys, rather than standing on mountains.

America started with *"When in the course of human Events, it becomes necessary for one People to dissolve the Political Bands which have connected them with another, and to assume among the Powers of the Earth, the separate and equal Station to which the Laws of Nature and of Nature's God entitle them"*. Today, the process by which America's *"Station"*, her sovereignty, can be lost has already begun, as leading Americans decided to ignore the God under Whom our Nation was created. The starting point of this great loss was her professing the faith of secular humanism with its definition of human life originating by Nature alone replacing her faith in the Creator God of her Fathers. The cheapening of human life this belief has caused in the consciousness of our society has set the nation on a path of self-destruction. With its Manifestoes, the religion of secular humanism has declared America's total independence from God and allegiance only to the created order - which is nothing but heathenism, according to the Holy Scriptures.

Whether we survive as the blessed Nation we inherited, or whether we perish ingloriously, depends on which of the following statements, both pregnant with meaning and consequences we ultimately accept and live by:

> *"...Laws of Nature and of Nature's God"* and *"Religious Humanists regard the universe as self-existing and not created... "*

Secularists are reading Reality wrong - it is Evil that is uncreated by God, not human beings. All the pain, injustice, poverty, illnesses, suffering and, finally, death plaguing human existence from the beginning of time first came into an once pristine, wholesome world, through the First Great Lie spoken by the Archenemy of life and believed by our first parents. *"Yea, hath God said... ?"* is how the Scriptures quote him in acting upon his rebellion. *"Ye shall not surely die"*, he added, "[for sinning] as the Creator said]". Possibly jealous about the exaltedness of the new beings bearing God's image and likeness, he wanted humankind to share his coming doom at the end of time - death.

Humanists, even if they mean well, are trying to do the right thing, but in the wrong, fatal way. The socio-political dogmas of Secular humanism can only increase the evils with their "correctives" for what ails humanity and Nature since our first parents "fell" for Satan's First Lie (The *"Fall"*). To cover up for all the evil inflicted on human life and Nature by the first - believed - lie, the *"Father of Lies"* who devised a second lie, naturalism, Darwinism, this time expressed by *"we begin with humans, not God, nature, not deity... No deity will save us, we must save ourselves."* The only truth these words acknowledge is that humanity and Nature do need salvation, which is something secular humanism has no resources or ability to provide.

Human words have meanings, but the Words coming from God have life in them for both people and nations. God's *Word* informs us that *"In Him is life"*, and *"...this life* [eternal life] is in His Son [the Incarnate God]". The God of the Pilgrims and of our Founders was the Incarnate God of the biblical teaching referred to by *"The Laws of Nature and Nature's God"* that introduced the charter of America. On that unforgettable, mild Sunday afternoon when I became personally acquainted with life as God created it, I discovered that these astounding words had the contour of the blank space so long empty in my "Puzzle That Is America". At that moment it became clear to me that the other over-whelming words, those of our Incarnate Creator - *"...whosoever liveth and believeth in me shall never die"* - also fitted neatly into the blank space. I placed them in, and my two puzzles were finally put together, the eternality for which we were created completing the panel of reality where humanity and Nature are portrayed by its all-knowing, all-seeing Creator.

The same way that only as Incarnate in human flesh does God save our souls, only as Creator God will He save America, if she so wills. At this critical time in the world's and America's history, our Creator waits, patiently, willingly, with His Father love in His heart and saving power in His hands, to see what is our will concerning both gifts of salvation.

A portentous choice was offered to the Israelite people by Moses, after God had him deliver them from their bondage, when just starting the people off as that other unique nation, a nation whose soul the Pilgrims desired as our sister-soul when conceiving America. Today, Moses' words proffered at a critical time for the Israelites are still to be heard echoing from the pages of the Judeo/Christian Scriptures through which God revealed Himself to the humanity He created. After thousands of years since these words were proclaimed on the plains of Moab, they have never lost their meaning and import - the same way Israel's identity as a nation has never been lost in the quicksand of time or through enemies' weapons, I fancy them as having been preserved especially for the ears of America today. Allow this 20th Century Pilgrim in America to repeat here the words of Moses, the George Washington of America's "sister-nation", for the sake of those deceived into keeping the Bible a closed book:

> *"I have set before you life and death, blessing and cursing;*
> *therefore choose life, that both thou and thy seed may live."*

THIRTEEN

A SURPRISING GIFT

"[W]e have no government armed with power capable of contending with human passion unbridled by morality and religion. Avarice, ambition, revenge, or gallantry, would break the strongest cord of our Constitution as a whale goes through a net. Our Constitution was made only for a moral and religious people. It is wholly inadequate to the government of any other"
(John Adams, America's second President)

"Before I [the Creator] *formed thee in the belly I knew thee"*
(Prophet Jeremiah)

America's unique soul, her true identity, has been sustained through the years by occasional and timely spiritual revivals. Spiritual revival is, basically, a renewed acknowledgement of God as our Creator and Savior and of His righteous demands upon those He created. It is unthinkable to expect God not to require from us the measure of divine image and likeness He imparted to us at our creation. Spiritual revival is the experiencing of personal redemption, the only gate to the restoration of humanity to its pristine state as originally created. The emotionalism and excesses experienced in these events are mostly by-products of religiosity. The redemption of humanity called for the Creator Himself to become a man, now with the wholesomeness and purity of "Man" as originally created, here to pay as man the righteous penalty for rebellion which is death in the Creator's book of laws, and rise again as *New Life* Creator. This is human history in time and space, not the history of religion. Nature itself, though not a living being and, thus, incapable of exercising any religion, is scheduled for redemption too; no religion will be required. The Judeo/Christian Scriptures know nothing of "comparative religions".

Only believers and unbelieving historians who care about all that pertains to Americana take the time to study these "religious events" we call spiritual revivals . Those who do this learn how these movements led large numbers of Americans back to the God of the Pilgrims and of the writers of our Declaration of Independence. Many of the human lightning rods of these movements of spiritual renewal were outstanding, cultured citizens, men like Jonathan Edwards, a theologian and philosopher; George Whitefield, who motivated the founding of over fifty colleges and universities; and many other prominent figures.

These times of spiritual renaissance came mostly when the moral standards of the Country reached a level low enough to threaten the life of America as a Republic governed by a freedom-enjoying people self-governing morally themselves. Our Nation would have never reached the high status she has enjoyed so far were it not for these "revivals of religion," as some historians generally refer to them, for America's ethos is innately connected with spirituality. History shows that in towns where these movements reached enough people, jails, salons, and brothels were closed; police forces where reduced to a minimum, and truly conservative representatives of the people were elected, thus assuring the continuation of a government "from the people, by the people, and for the people". The spiritual revivals raising the moral standards of the country made it possible for America to keep this feature of her identity and uniqueness. History has proven over and over again how right John Adams, Washington, Lincoln, and many others in the Nation's leadership were when warning Americans of the disastrous consequences to America for turning their backs on her Fathers' God. To understand exactly what they meant, we have to keep in mind how our

Founders defined religion. By "True Religion" they didn't mean a particular denomination considered to be the true one by them. The new nation was to be composed of adherents to all religions or none, or they wouldn't have been forming a nation where freedom reigned, not a King.

History proves also that America's leaders, like John Adams, knew their Bibles; what they said or wrote concerning the connection between spirituality and morals and a nation's well-being and success is one of the truths the Judeo/Christian Scriptures alludes to when dealing with world history. Knowing the contents of the Bible as they did, I wonder what they would say about the present moral and political state of America, especially in being aware of the fulfilled biblical prophecies about the fate of God-defying nations.

A spiritual awakening in America and the world has never been needed with as much urgency as it is today. A Nation such as ours, born free and living to promote freedom now, allowing herself to be enslaved by secularism; a Nation conceived and reared "under God" now affronting the Creator of Life by killing, so far, fifty millions of her children in their mothers' wombs; openly demonstrating immoral behaviors of the ugliest sorts; condoning and legalizing abortion and pornography and even profiting from them - cannot stay unpunished for too long. One must wonder whether there is enough revival-generating repentance left on the part of a society whose conscience has been so profoundly seared. Speaking for myself and for other students of biblical prophecies whose work I am familiar with, it is very possible that America has passed the point where she can still hear the alarm sounding the saving time for spiritual awakening. Americans must be prepared for the two contingencies - the *"latter rains",* blessings, of the biblical prophetic utterances following a presently protracted spiritual revival, or a righteous God's punishment for the grievous sins which modern society is openly committing and its rulers are irresponsibly condoning.

How then are we to live is such a declining Country? What are we to do, in these disturbing days threatening the dissolution of an once amiable Nation blessed with the right habitat for human beings to live and thrive?

I shall be forever grateful for what I call the "natural habitat" for human living which America's Fathers created in this Nation. It was in such a favorable atmosphere to which this American By Choice was made welcome that he learned the true meaning of human life, even while searching for America's secret of greatness. And from this lesson I learned another great truth, a corollary one about the true meaning and worth of life as having been created by an All-knowing Creator. This experience surprised me with a gift worth many times over the other gifts America has given me, such as the sharing of her values, her life amenities, her freedom, and incentives to succeed in life. If receiving the first gift overwhelmed me with gratitude, taking possession of the second one at first made me speechless for a while for its richness, until I predisposed myself to write this book in seeking to recover my voice in time to talk about this extraordinary gift and how its practical use can revolutionize one's life. It did mine. And, if doing the same to enough of us, we shall be able together to bring America back to the safety of the path she once treaded.

What I further discovered when finding the answers to both life's and America's puzzles is this: though as a Nation, America might never recover from her present malady; though she might never choose to recover the threefold cord that has sustained her for so long - our Founders Creator God; right habitat for humans, with the welcomed Presence of God in her midst through her willingness to stay a Nation Under God might be extinguished in a cultural atmosphere of unbelief; though it is very possible that all these negatives things become irreversible, even sooner than we expect, as a believer, I shall still carry with me that life-friendly atmosphere still producing around and within me my own right habitat for human living. For the faith of our Nation's Fathers which conditioned her to be the right venue for her children's *"pursuit of happiness"*, in the words of our Declaration of Independence, is the same faith that can condition the individual, to keep on living *"more abundantly"*, as the Judeo/Christian Scriptures describes a believer's life. And, as I learned previously, this abundant life will go on forever.

With the few remaining chapters of this book I'll be sharing with the reader the life-enriching results of making the learning experience I went through my day-to-day philosophy of living. I'll be telling how my attitude toward myself, in my few successes and many failures, toward God and others, toward the good things in life and the many unavoidable bad things, has changed for the better; how a true understanding of life, of myself, God, and the world He created gives a person the proper perspective needed to establish the right priorities - and the peace of mind that comes from this; how the realization of where you come from as a human being and where you are going from here, the meaning of life and the purpose for your existence, can, increasingly, make your earthly life worth living, "more abundant" indeed; how the anticipation of seeing, hearing, and entering into the inexpressible good things *"prepared for those who love God"* gives a new spring to your steps on the path of life even when the way is stony, dark, or unpleasant. No, this is not "make believe," or a product manufactured by positive thinking. This is for real. I am not alone in this. Many others have experienced this phenomenon before me. I find myself often shouting for joy with the discovery of new sources of joyful living and, wanting to share them, scrambling to find the right words to express the feeling and insights.

What you'll be reading here is fully covered in the Judeo/Christian Scriptures, where they are written in the most exquisite form and often in symbols, the helpful devices which the omniscient Writer uses to cause us to visualize something with no point of reference in what we experience so early in our earthly life designed for eternity.

The Bible shows how even on earth human lives can imbibe more of God's Own life which was once breathed into "Man". This possibility comes with your spiritual rebirth through personal redemption. *"In Him is Life... in Him we live, and move, and have our being"* the Scriptures teaches us. Though lost through rebellion, life as originally created can be recovered in rebirth through regeneration. The effects of this God-imparted growing Godliness out of regeneration can be felt daily in homes, in the market place, and in the corridors of power. This is not a matter of just religion, unless we are now aware of the true meaning of our Nation's Founders' "True Religion" which has to do with *"God's Nature and Nature's God"* - that is, with reality itself.

FOURTEEN

RELIGION OF LIFE?

"Sing them over again to me, Wonderful words of Life;
Let me more of their beauty see, Wonderful words of Life.
Words of life and beauty teach me faith and duty;
Beautiful words, wonderful words,
Wonderful words of life!" (Hymn writer P. P. Bliss)

"... the words that speak I unto you, they are spirit,
and they are life". (The Incarnate Life's Redeemer)

This might come as a surprise to most skeptics, but the Bible is basically a long treatise on human life and our relationship with its Creator. The Creator of Life and its Incarnate Redeemer never founded a religion. The "Word of God", the Bible, informs us, after describing our Savior's resurrection and temporary physical departure from this world, that those who believed in Him were called Followers of The Way. This imperishable Book is about life, about people and their Creator. Read it, as I learned to, in order to meet your personal need of finding truth - Truth with a capital "T" - about life, about the world it populates and the Creator of these realities, and you'll soon discover that the Bible is a complete Life Manual.

Like most people who do not take the time to read the Bible, humbly, honestly seeking to meet their personal need for Truth, to secular humanism's worldview, the Judeo/Christian Scriptures is just another book on religion.

The Judeo/Christian Scriptures doesn't present to us a forum where we can find out which religion is "right". You can find in it the real truth about yourself, about the world, evil, sin, doubts, time, and timeless infinity. What is more importantly practical, it shows you how to satisfy your yearning for purity, for goodness, beauty, and for meaning in life, whenever you find yourself personally desiring these things. Read it as a book that deals with these realities and you'll soon discover that the Bible doesn't teach one more religion to be added to the growing roster of them. You'll find out also that the Bible addresses the individual, not society. Put your name as the addressee of its commands, instructions and warnings and you'll quickly find that out.

Despite its friendly name, to secular humanism the prevailing religion of our days, the individual person is simply another "species" in the animal family, not a precious and unique, single entity housing an eternal soul. That is why philosophically and politically, secular humanists do not emphasize the individual, but the society by which he is influenced and which he helps create. In the secular humanist's worldview, the person, both the unborn and the living, soulless as per their religious doctrines, is spendable for the sake of an imaginable "good" sought to benefiting society as a whole - the good without God which mostly results in evil. That has been, for years now, the political philosophy behind our children's textbooks. This is what results in Socialism and Statism, the forces ignoring and enslaving the single individual. That is the ideology which has already brought so much grief and death to the world and is now threatening to devastate America. And that's one of the reasons why adherents of secular humanism want the Bible taken away from students', teachers' and journalists' and magistrates' desks. Having become itself a religion, it wants no competition.

By default, the Bible exposes humanism as a self-righteous religion. Even if sincere in its proposals about how to correct what is wrong in human society, its proposed means to accomplish this is social, economical fallacies, since in their relativism right and wrong are labeled so by the variableness of circumstances. With so inconsistent a standard, secular humanism finds nothing wrong with the individual, only the society which the individual lives in. But the Bible shows the finger of the God of Absolutes pointing to me as an individual, exposing what is not right with me, rather than what is not right with my society. What is really wrong in society is discovered as the context of what is wrong with the single individual not pursuing Godliness.

Not believing in the only existing source of pure good - God - and of unmistakable evil - the Chief Life's Enemy, secular humanism doesn't consider the person and what is actually wrong with each single individual. Thus, whatever humanism proposes of good doesn't come to you in individual portions. Because they cater to society as a whole, what they have of good - i.e., that which they determine as good within the relativism of their dogmas - must come in bulk, to be impersonally, politically distributed. And their concern is primarily for the physical, the material, not the whole of human reality. Not so with the teaching found in the book authored by the One who authored reality itself. Human life's redemption from what disfigured it from its originally created wholesomeness is its central theme. Whatever good that is to come to society must come from God, its true source, through the instrumentality of those who love God. That's why the Savior resumed all the teaching of *"the laws and the prophets"* into a single clause He called also a law, *"love God above all things and your neighbor as thyself"* and the principle this law establishes: *"Seek ye first the Kingdom of God and His righteousness and all things shall be added unto you"*. And that's why charity, now politically called "welfare" is a duty of people, not of the state, a simple truth perennially absent from political platforms and even religious forums.

This circumspectful living, as C.S. Lewis would have the redeemed to live, is the theme for the remaining few chapters of this book. As that famous Christian apologist characterizes that mode of living in his autobiography which he titled *Surprised by Joy*, that circumspection is interspersed with much joy - *"joy unspeakable and full of glory"* as Peter, the fisherman turned Apostle, puts it. While writing the rest of this book, again, I shall still be shunning preaching, though I might be thought of as doing that since we cannot escape the confining vocabulary of religion in expressing experiential facts having to do with the soul. Anything that can be said about how life ought to be lived must of necessity suggest religion, since human life was conceived in the Creator's mind, crafted by His hands, and having His Own life breathed in. But breathing is not a religious act in the human religions' sense of the word, and it is in one's breathing that laymen like me detect the presence of life, though life is really the unseen presence of our Creator Himself within us - or not in us, depending on our own choice. We should never allow the word "God" to suggest religion, but Reality. That is how I can be intellectually honest in saying that I shall be commenting on how we ought to live in our changing nation and changing world without appealing to religion.

FIFTEEN

KNOWLEDGE OR WISDOM?
OR, IS THAT ALL?

"Vanity of vanities, saith the Preacher. vanity of vanities; all is vanity. What a profit hath a man of all his labour which he taketh under the sun?" (Ecclesiastes)

*"...we speak wisdom ...not yet the wisdom of this world,
nor of the princes of this world, that come to nought:
but we speak of God in a mystery, even the hidden wisdom,
which God ordained before the world unto our glory:
which none of the princes of this world knew:
for had they known it they would not have crucified
the Lord of glory."* (The Apostle Paul)

*"The thief cometh not, but for the steal, and to kill, and to destroy:
I am come that they might have life, and that they might have it
more abundantly"* (God Incarnate)

Because I promised not to do something I am not qualified to do - preach - I was, at first, inclined not to include this chapter in my book. But I'll have to, for the trend of the book's message will be broken without it. I ask you to read it as a soliloquy - just an old man enthralled with the grandeur of life, with God, with the infinity of his discoveries, talking to himself about them.

It is not going to be easy for anyone to believe this story about one of my life experiences as a youth. But the tale is true. In my early teens, while still in my native Country, I was employed by a bank for a while. At the end of the week, my manager would put together in a good-sized bundle, a large number of bills amounting to many thousands of dollars. He had the parcel tied with strings and ordered two of us, both kids, to take the money downtown, to the bank's main office, which was located a long distance from where we set out. We carried the money by hand, traveling on public transportation which was, then, a noisy street-car built and run by the British.

Being very poor and knowing the quite large amount of money we had temporarily in our power, we felt very important, and, at the same time, quite frolicsome. We played with the parcel of money as we did with soccer balls which we used to make out of rags. The passers-by never realized the fortune we were kicking around in the middle of the street or casually tossing to each other while walking to and from the "tram" station. The two of us laughed heartily, enjoying our secret as we rode the trolley. It would be many years before I was to learn the English idiomatic expression fitting to that occasion - I would have said then that we "had a ball!". To this day, this English colloquialism reminds me of that rare experience. And it also pictures to me the carelessness with which we are inclined to handle the richness of life, especially in a prosperous country like America.

At that time I didn't contest the wisdom of my employers in using two kids instead of an armored truck to transfer cash. I didn't know any better myself. Actually, I never saw any of those intimidating valuables-carrying vehicles until I came to America. I figured that my boss must have concluded, in his own wisdom, that robbers would never guess what was inside the "ball" we played with. Wisdom which I do contest today is the much touted wisdom of King Solomon. How did a man declared to be the wisest among men end up doing so many ludicrous things as he did? I feel we can be justified, with humor and a tiny bit of wisdom of my own, in ribbing him for some of those reckless decisions of his - like accumulating hundreds of wives and building altars to the heathen gods they worshipped. And to further cater to his rampant sensuality, he got himself a bevy of concubines on the side!

Since coming to this country, I have learned what I think is one of the best vehicles of literary humor in the English-speaking world - limericks. Just for fun, I have made a hobby of writing such piquant verses myself. I even published a little book grouping a bunch of them. After hearing about a boy who misspelled the word "concubine" during a Sunday School lesson, I could not keep myself from adding one more limerick to my collection. I usually let my wife Olivia (do I have to name her as if I have more than one wife myself?) find titles for them. She entitled this one "Divines' Concubines":

A kid, I hear via grape-vines,
Beats King Solomon and all his divines.
Those gents' wisdom he excels
Even when he misspells:
"Besides wives, the King had porcupines."

Judging by our modern secular values, Solomon had everything supposedly capable of making the wisest of men also the happiest of them all. But that is not what you learn from reading some of the things he wrote and from what we know about his life. Something was missing in his rich portfolio of knowledge, something that would have caused him to contentedly enjoy his famous collection of good things - his fame, power, and wealth. The poor man didn't seem to know enough to know, as even I suspected in my early teens, that playing with a parcel of riches is not a wise thing to do. It doesn't satisfy one's soul, even if you are temporarily "having a ball".

Though Solomon started well, later in life he seems to have become oblivious to the truth that collecting gold and wives and playing King or any other such games only enriches moments, not a lifetime. Besides, since he knew so much, he should have known that human life survives the grave, and the body in which it lives shouldn't be used as a toy. He didn't seem to know that by giving in to unrestrained sensuality he could get unexpectedly hurt by "porcupines' " sharp quills, especially in old age, as actually happened to him. He was not even wise enough to live by his own many counsels, such as he wrote in Proverbs, *"Hast thou found honey? Eat so much as is sufficient for thee, lest thou be filled therewith, and vomit it"*. The choices Solomon made in his life tell us that he didn't seem to have learned how to enjoy and be content with pleasures which do not become sharp quills and don't cause bellyaches. He didn't seem to know the portentous meaning of the fact that his life originated in a righteous God - the truly regal status of a soul aware of its innate glory.

Solomon's philosophy of life is a picture of knowledgeable, modern Western atheists and deists always wishing for something new and earthly *"under the sun"* with which to extract some meaning to life independent from the Creator of life. Like Solomon, they don't realize that all earthly things either melt or harden under the sun. That is one of the *"things"* which has not changed in this 21st Century. For all practical purposes, many of us are emulating Solomon's actual life, and not the wisdom which his writings teach. Like that Jewish King, what is important enough for many of us to occupy ourselves with is that which is "under the sun", visible and warm to our senses. The unseen, the spiritual, though as much real as love and as much sure as physical death in its day-and-night shadowy presence, is carelessly considered to be only an appendix to reality, an after-thought that is not to be expressed too often, and certainly not, in public. It is a "private matter" and shouldn't be brought out before the court of intellectual, political, or cultural correctness.

All of us have inherited from the Fall a tendency to be more concerned with our own life's ongoing physical requirements for gratification, though for many of us, with some added immaterial or intellectual interests which we pursue for inspirational purposes. Our natural inclination is to expect to secure only from earthly sources all that we need for personal success so as to make our living circumstances as pleasurable as possible. With the profusion of material resources we have today, even sensibility is becoming, to some of us, a supplement one can, somehow, live without. Concerns with the here-and-now making up the common denominator in most everything we read, hear, and watch today, demonstrates well the existentialism of our present culture. Sadly, what is emphasized in our considerations even when some of us theologize and preach about Heaven is mostly what has to do with the earthly menu for earthly living, finite things which only meet temporary needs and wants. The topics of most books and conversations are restricted to finitudes even when we put God in the picture. The noxious fall-out of man-centeredness coming from the explosion of secular humanism in our era seems to cover not only the marketplace and the academic and political establishments, but even homes, pulpits, and pews.

This is, perhaps, because today, more than ever, we learn about life through the eyes and think about what we learn with our feelings. The result of this inadvertently imbibed secularism is that we look at all that pertains to earthly living disconnected from our souls, from spirituality. What we learn thus is not to be viewed under heavenly, eternal lighting so that it might be properly studied, evaluated, and guiltlessly, joyfully, lived out. In our present atmosphere of naturalism, there seems to be a diminishing interest in the spiritual and post-mortem aspects of reality, though life is as short as eternity is immeasurably long.

What truly gives life its worth, meaning, and purpose, both in time and eternity - spiritual things, the joys of the soul, rather than bodily pleasures - is taken as a mere utilitarian truth to be reluctantly added to the temporary gratifications of earthly living. The shortness of life is becoming the very reason for the foolhardiness of such unintelligent, existential life style.

Of late, this seems to be true even when the subject is personal salvation. Despite the cosmic relevance of creation and redemption which lends meaning and worth to life, a heaven to go to eventually is often perceived as just the icing on the cake, giving earthly living a better taste. Yet, there is more, oh! so much more to salvation than "a pie in the sky when you die" of the mocking skeptic, even if we take the pie for a metaphor making of it pearly gates and streets of gold.

Since the Fall, humanity has acquired an instinctive inclination toward a form of mild existentialism. Our culture's growing belief in naturalism encourages this tendency to live as if temporal things and earthly accomplishments are the only empirical sources of life's meaningfulness and satisfaction available to us. It seems that, though adults, we avoid considering that the joys of kicking around packages of temporary valuables for too long will eventually cease when the parcel is torn and its contents are spilled under the sun. Yet, deep down, we know that that is not all there is to reality; that though we try to forget, makeshift balls will surely come apart someday. Like Solomon, who let human knowledge guide his life while disregarding the wisdom of his God-given privilege of abstaining from evils, we, too, might at any time find ourselves looking at our losses and exclaiming, pathetically, "Vanity of vanity; all is vanity!". Or, less poetically and more to the point, "Is that all there is to life?" Solomon is a vivid example of what famous or accomplished people experience as a surprising fact of life - there is nothing but disappointment waiting at the summit of earthly success reached without God.

Like Solomon, all of us can easily become mere apathetic theists even while thinking of ourselves as religious enough, as if simply by choosing and following a religion we can live life as life created in the image and likeness of God should be like. I think of one who is a believer and an existentialist at the same time to be a "hybrid theist". Judging by his writings and behavior, Solomon became one of those hybrids, though this seems to have never occurred to him. Something was missing in the otherwise wise (no pun intended) King's perceptions. Whatever their doctrinal stand, hybrid theists travel the same life highway taken by agnostics and atheists. Their destination is the same, for doctrines themselves, even the soundest ones, cannot save even the best of theoreticians in the absence of, in the words of our Savior, a "childlike faith" implementing consonant works. Though along the road the scenery is, for a time, pleasant and exciting to their senses, like that of kids kicking around a package with money, it actually leads to Bunyan's City of Destruction, either at the very next bend or at its unavoidable final dead-end. This is true whatever dogmas of their religion or theistic philosophy of life they hold, and whether these dogmas are true or false. I cannot think of a more somber thought than to realize that that irreversible event at life's end - bodily death - can happen at any time without our having learned to connect every aspect of life to eternity. This telling possibility is not easily noticed through the blurriness of materialism. Only eyes purposely turned toward eternity can see it.

As with Solomon, in America, with all our prosperity, we can easily fail to acquire simple things such as common sense, the by-product of wisdom which human passions can easily extinguish. Yet, it is not easy to live without a daily dose of this life-staple. This is especially true in today's world shaped by an abundance of knowledge and magic-like technology. Good sense alone should be able to keep us from failing to consider the possibility of a higher purpose for our being born than just existing. Good judgment should be reminding us of the high worth this consideration gives to life and the unfortunate consequences of its devaluation.

Human life is too intense, too far-reaching and complex, to be taken as just a product of mindless, accidental happenstance, and not as a purposeful creation conceived and crafted by a transcendental and all-knowing, creative intelligence. This should be easily perceived even by irreligious persons. Creationism presents a sufficient, bona fide explanation of life's origin even if naturalists think of it as a delusion of an old-fashioned set of religious beliefs which they consider "unscientific"; even if atheists insist that it is like a bad virus that should be removed from modern, computer-like minds. Creationism, like transcendence, ought to be to Reason the most obvious explanation of reality, especially to scientists, and particularly to those delving into the mysteries of quantum.

Our culture's foolhardiness in still kicking the riches of life around in such a time as ours is greater than that of Solomon or that of two kids playing soccer with a paper ball filled with money on the streets of a "third-world Country". The extent of what Solomon knew, though we are told that he mastered all the knowledge of his time, can hardly be compared with the incredible knowledge our civilization has now secured. Yet, as with Solomon, materialism is pandemic today, and sensuality and heretical beliefs proliferate under the sun, and the cry of "Vanity of vanity; all is vanity" is heard wherever meaninglessness has found depressions like running water finds hollows in the ground. Like Solomon, who, despite his abundant knowledge, adopted the heathen cruelty of burning his living children before a pagan god, our culture, too, has made life that cheap. In our 21st Century uncivil civilization, we are heartlessly sacrificing living babies on the humanist altar - the wombs of their would-be mothers - rebelliously denying that both offering and altar are designed by a holy Creator, and *"fearfully and wonderfully made"* as the Bible describes life. And that most unwise of all deeds is being sanctioned and promoted by our modern King Solomons from the same seats of power from which truly wise Americans of the past honored God as Creator, and His human creation as sacred.

In our day and age we can do no wiser thing if we are to live our life in the fullness of its meaning and worthiness than to reach for our copy of the Judeo-Christian Holy Scriptures, the Book which our culture has foolishly replaced in our schools and homes with *The Origin of Species*. Its profound, true wisdom, which surpasses knowledge in richness of living, is the active answer in the solution that can wash our minds clean of naturalism's poisonous delusions; it will start us out on our journey toward the *"abundant life"* which the Creator of life promised everyone of us with His Own human lips as God Incarnate. God's Holy Spirit will do the rest.

SIXTEEN

WHO AM I AND
WHO ARE YOU?
(OR, "REPENTANCE UNTO LIFE")

"When I consider thy heavens, the work of thy fingers, the moon and the stars which thou hast ordained; what is man, that thou are mindful of him? and the son of man, that thou visitest him? For thou madest him a little lower than the angels, and hast crowned him with glory and honor." (The Psalms)

"Scientific measurements indicate that we are moving even when we are standing still. The surface of the earth at the equator rotates at about 1,000 miles per hour. The earth is orbiting the sun at about 67,000 miles per hour. Our solar system whirls around the center of our galaxy at 490,000 miles per hour and it zooms along at 43,000 miles per hour in the direction of the star Vega in the constellation Lyra. But that's not all. Our Milky Way galaxy is hurtling through space at 1.3 million miles per hour. A man lying on his back in a quiet park on a cloudless summer day may feel as though all time and movement have stopped under the hot rays of a noonday sun. But the scientist and the godly person know otherwise. Just as we are hurtling through the heavens at unimaginable speeds, so too we are moving from here to eternity." (MRD II, in Daily Bread).

Think about what those who know teach us, like the mind-boggling fact that there are 69 suns in the Milky Way galaxy for each living human being and 8 galaxies for each one of us living today. Then imagine yourself being the one lying on your back on that cloudless summer day, thinking about those unbelievable features of such huge bodies of matter, you being aware that the same matter is what makes up your body. Measured for size against the grandeur of the universe cradling us, we are much, much smaller than a fly measured against the elephant it rides on. If you wonder how and why puny-sized human beings, though dwarfed exponentially by the enormity of sizes and distances and numbers which scientists keep discovering in the cosmos, are, nonetheless, capable of realizing and appraising some of that vastness; if you wonder how and why all that bounteous astronomic reality can be apprehended by your perishable three-pound brain; and if after learning of such wonders you are still foolish enough to think that all this enormity, complexity, beauty, and a mind capable of absorbing it all just happened accidentally; if you fail to conclude, humbly and reverently, that there must be a mighty power exercised by an omniscient mind maintaining these wonders which He deliberately, purposely created, you have been disastrously infected by the soul-destroying concept of life and the world held by our otherwise knowledgeable but proud age. And by this failure you are forfeiting your own place and role in the life-enriching purpose for Creation, for all that you see, and cannot yet see, was created with you in mind! (This is another life-changing truth you can only learn from the Holy Scriptures). You would have then be using your free-will, one of your likenesses to your Creator, to cause yourself the greatest of all losses a human being can suffer - and that, for eternity - for God respects your will in the same way He demands of us to revere His.

As the initial ripple on the sea formed by the fall of a pebble might, miles and days later, cause a tidal wave; as the pin-sized matter from which cosmologists insist the whole universe burst into being, so are you and me. We are that pebble, we are that microscopic matter. But our smallness is in that of the body alone, and even that perishable body is scheduled to be reconstituted to perfection someday at the *"Last Resurrection"*, and, then, to *"die no more"*. You'll find out these awesome truths about God, humanity, and the world of their habitation when, open-mindedly, you read the Judeo/Christian Scriptures. You'll find out also, for your circumspection and joy in believing, that, like C. S. Lewis' Narnia, you are *"bigger inside than outside."*

Who am I? Who are you? Contrary to the conventional academic beliefs, contrary to what you were taught in school, gleaned often from television and read in most books and magazines today; like the universe your body is a part of, you are a purposefully created being yourself. In the words of the Bible, just like the world, you, too, were *"wonderfully made"*. You were in God's mind, the mind capable of creating so vast and magnificent universe, *before* you were conceived in the womb. You were crafted with objectives which dwarf in grandeur and marvels the sizes of celestial matter and lengths of distances. It stands to reason that the Creator must be above His Creation in grandeur too, and so are you as created in the Creator's Own image and likeness. That makes you an entity of inestimable worth. You are actually worth *"more than the whole world"*. This appraisal came from the holy lips of the Creator of life Himself, while living physically on earth in His astonishing mission of restoring humanity to the fullness of His divine image and likeness.

Think of it: all this is true about you, whoever you are by gender, age, nationality, color, or status - whether you are handsome, ugly, sick, healthy, rich or poor. As a human being, you are the greatest wonder among all created wonders. From the day the wonder of you was conceived in the womb of your mother, you have been standing at the edge of the sea of eternity where incorporeal and physical wonders lie in their fullness. And you have been designed to participate in them someday, with all your senses then properly honed, like those of their Creator, to fully take in and rejoice in them. And because those wonders were created for you, according to the

Holy Scriptures, you don't have to begrudge them. Because you bear the image and likeness of the Creator, you are suited to share for all eternity, if you so choose, the baffling wonder of God's very life, and with His life, things more marvelous than huge bodies, enormous speeds, and indescribable beauty. And you and I were created and fitted to experience and be part of these wonders.

God, with His superb creativity and might which only His great love for us can match, has made all the necessary preparation for us, His likenesses, to contemplate those wonders and complement them in His eternal presence; all this for the delight of our souls and of His own divine heart. Through His incarnation and work of atonement He has made us able to escape the prison of sin, time, and limitations which constrains us now. Before long, we shall find ourselves in what can only be described as another dimension of reality where unlimitedness is in the very air we will breathe. In that spatial boundlessness, with the final redemption of Humanity and Nature completed as planned, the divine-like joy for which we were created is abundant and everlasting. *"...And these things I speak in the world, that they might have my joy fulfilled in themselves"*, was the way the Incarnate God alludes to that reality to His disciples, as well as *"to them also which shall believe on Me through their* [His Disciples'] *words..."*. *"Joy unspeakable and full of glory"*, was the way the Apostle Paul further described that joy, a depiction so rich in meaning as to be often wrongly taken by many as mere poetical license. The fact that the Incarnate God said these words in a prayer, making of them a petition only hours before He was to shed His atoning blood, vastly enhances the truth and significance of His words. For this prayer, made by the Human Person of the Godhead to the Father-God can't possibly be unanswered.

Our brain, eyes, and ears are still incapable of fully apprehending so transcendental a reality in God's drama of Creation and Redemption whose final chapter is yet to be enacted. Because of this, He has it written about it in simple, invitingly human words: "... *Since the beginning of the world men have not heard, nor perceived by the ear, neither hath the eye seen, O God, beside thee, what he hath prepared for him that waiteth for him* [God]". That's how Isaiah, the Prophet, foresaw this cosmic phenomenon. On this side of our Redeemer's all-renewing resurrection, the formerly unbelieving Saul, later Apostle Paul and one of the amanuenses used by the Author of the Holy Scriptures, puts it in more contemporary language: "*...as it is written, Eye hath not seen, nor ear heard, neither have entered into the heart of man, the things which God hath prepared for them that love him.*" What those "things" are in kind only God knows for sure. Even if we could guess what they are by using what we know of good as a point of reference, I suspect our Creator would still keep them a temporary secret. It seems He loves to surprise His twice-born children the way a human father does in keeping a child from learning what is in the box until the actual birthday. But He made sure we learn, as expectant children, that pure, unalloyed joy is what those "things" will give to those who love Him. All that goodness and beauty can be summarized with one single word: Life. Life as first conceived in God's mind as an extension of His Own life and shared with our first parents.

Since the beginning of time, philosophers and theologians (once upon a time these two disciplines were one and the same) have been making intellectual sorties into God's treasury of knowledge. If those promises sound tantalizing to us in our present limitedness and with our current bent to sinning, it is because we instinctively know that those things must be the fruition of what we know of goodness, justice, love, and beauty - the gifts of divine image and likeness graciously left in our consciousness by our Creator, samplings of divine attributes virtually coded in our souls. What we know and sense about these tokens of the divine enabling of us to appreciate and long for them all the more, gives us a foretaste of their fullness, even if "*as in a glass*", in the words of the Bible. Their presence within our inner being, though only small samplings now, speaks to us of pure joy and virtuous pleasures to be perfected someday when time, sin, and death no longer have their place in the reality of things, and human lusts no longer corrupt that "unspeakable joy".

When incarnate in human flesh for His cosmic mission of redeeming humanity and Nature, our Creator changed not only history, but the believer's concept of time, human life, and our all-important relationships with God, one another, and the matter we are housed in. Having at the beginning spurned God by believing the First Great Lie, humanity was given, at the Cross, the opportunity to replace the first belief with a second one - this time a belief in an eternal truth, not a lie. The events of the Incarnation and the Resurrection are real historical occurrences, no matter if atheists and skeptics call them a myth. In the words of the Bible, words which match human experience, the first belief took humanity to the *"way that leads unto death"*, and the second to the way that *"leads unto life"*.

At the Cross, a vista of a New World was presented to humanity through the open gates of Redemption. There, at Golgotha, a distinct line was drawn, visible only to the eyes of faith, since *"the just* (or 'the justified', in another rendering of this scriptural verse) *shall live by faith"* . This line both separates, and, paradoxically, joins together two kingdoms, two realms - the Kingdom of Time and the Kingdom of Eternity, what our Savior called the kingdom of Man and the Kingdom of God. A mystery, this is the double-faced news of the *"gospel of the Kingdom"* which the Savior of humanity *"went about preaching"* - the Kingdom He proclaimed as already belonging to innocent children but one that we should pray that it might come; the peculiar Kingdom which, He explained, *"is already within* [in the midst of] *you* [who love me]", for it is the Creator and Redeemer of life's Own life *"in you"* as later elucidated by the Apostles. This is the Kingdom which, if you *"seek above all things, everything* [else] *will be added unto you"* - the Gospel of the Kingdom which the conceivers of our Nation were to take for principles applying to our nation too, as long as she remained "Under God". That is what enabled us, in our polity designed for a dual citizenship, to enjoy a standard of living and freedom as never experienced by other countries before, while waiting for God's Eternal Kingdom to be established, as promised - the eternal Kingdom of a truly united nations pragmatically, finally, Under God also.

Even theologians of today for whom theology is a branch of philosophy, as much as philosophers for whom philosophy is to fully encompass all there is about the theme of God and salvation, cannot fathom this *"mystery of the Kingdom of God"* with the mind alone. The Kingdom which our Savior "went about preaching" cannot be perceived without the eyesight provided by that *"childlike faith"*. But intellectuals are not alone in this selective blindness. At first, His Own disciples also failed to see it until our Savior's resurrection, after He died a death that should have been our death. The Bible tells us that, even after three years of constant teaching and convincing show-and-tell events, all His Disciples, fishermen and tax-collectors alike, left Him; they *"fled"* as it was predicted centuries before the Crucifixion. In its strict honesty, the Bible even reports to us that Peter - later St. Peter - actually denied knowing the rejected King of God's Kingdom, not once, but three times. Just before writing this chapter, I read again the biblical account of those first days and months following the Savior's death and resurrection. A brief reference to the contents of these passages will greatly help me make the point of this Chapter:

Our God and Creator, Incarnate in human flesh, had just been crucified. His Jewish disciples were stunned at such a tragic event involving another Jew, a young man Who, though exhibiting divine attributes, was expected to be by now challenging the Roman occupation of their land; instead, He died with the excruciating pain of crucifixion at the young age of 33. His followers were having quite a time in putting things together. After all, hadn't He often referred to Himself as the prophesied coming Messiah, their conquering King of a coming, righteous kingdom?

After his potential earthly king died, a stricken Peter had left the diabolical Roman scene of crucifixion with a resigned, "[Well], *I'll go* [back] *fishing*". Even later on, after knowing about his Master's overcoming death and, as foretold, resurrection from His stony tomb, the stubborn fisherman's eyes were still closed to the exhilarating truth he and the world were about to be exposed to. He was back to fishing at the lake when his resurrected Master called from the shore for His disciples to join Him for a breakfast of fried fish and bread which He prepared Himself. Peter, who had three times denied Him, had to be asked three times whether he still loved the King who was not crowned, this, apparently, so that the fisherman might know for sure that he did love Him and was forgiven for his previous threefold denial. Later, in the account of the events that followed that transforming experience, Simon Peter, now invisibly garbed in apostolic vestments in place of his fisherman's clothes, was a guest in the home of another Simon, a man whose profession Judaism loathed - for what he did for a living was not really "kosher". Since made a *"fisher of men"* for passing the love-test, Peter was having a crash course on the difference between religion and The Way of Life which his Teacher taught, the practical difference between the Kingdom of Man and the Kingdom of God. Now, at the home of Simon, the tanner, while hungry and waiting to be served another breakfast, the disciple-turned-Apostle was having a vision of a *"sheet knit at the four corners"* loaded with, for a Jew like him, *"unclean"* food. A voice from heaven was telling him to eat it, for God *"hath cleansed it."* Three times the sheet had to be lowered down to him; three times the voice ordered him to eat his religiously unlawful food, apparently because of Peter responding to the thrice given orders by beating his faithful Jewish chest, exclaiming, *"Not so, Lord... I have never eaten anything that is unclean."*

That was precisely the time when three men of the "wrong race" - Gentiles - showed up at the tanner's house looking for Peter, with an invitation to travel somewhere with them, to visit with another Gentile - of all things, a Roman centurion, a soldier whose job was to keep Israelites like him under the servitude of Rome. Even then, the recalcitrant Jew *"doubted in himself what this vision which he had should mean"*, a vision whose meaning you and I can quickly understand just by reading about it and knowing some basic things about Jewishness.

This story about God's fisherman, with its enormous historical and theological significance, ends up with Peter now in the home of the Roman centurion. This Gentile is described as *"a devout man, and one that feared God with all his house, who gave much alms to the people, and prayed to God alway"*. It was only after Peter introduced his refused Jewish King to the centurion and his household as Redeemer and Savior, and witnessed God's Spirit falling on them as He did on the disciples on the day of Pentecost, that the Apostle was able to start seeing that hardly visible line between the two kingdoms. When explaining to his Jewish brethren the reason for his breach of the Jewish religion's laws, Peter's now humbled reasoning and understanding were duly expressed: *"Who was I to withstanding God?"*. And his *"contending"* Jewish brethren were the ones who saw the light which Peter finally perceived: *"Then hath God also to the Gentiles granted **repentance unto life**"*. And here is my point in bringing out this biblical passages: the *repentance* required of a seeker of salvation, of redemption, was unto **life** - the *"granting"* was not *"unto"* a new religion or to just gain a place in Heaven, but unto life, the Savior's "Way of Life".

And there it was, the paradoxical line both separating and connecting the Kingdom of Man to God's Kingdom, what was called religion, to life, the *"the Gospel of the Kindgom"*. From then on the followers of the Incarnate God were to preach repentance unto life, life as originally created and now available again through God's Incarnation and the Cross; repentance from a life in rebellion and sin leading to death, or, like the Roman centurion whose good deeds would still keep him lifeless while still not redeemed by a life-giving Savior, into the new life offered by the *"Gospel of Life"*; repentance unto a life of growth by His grace into the fullness of God's image, likeness, and eternal life; repentance as the first step in the "way of holiness" predicted by the Old Testament prophets.

Both Israelites and Gentiles, now followers of the resurrected Creator of life were considered at the beginning of the year 33 A.D. not Jews and Christians, but as "Followers of the Way". And that "way" of life was the very "Gospel" of the "First Comers" to America, the Pilgrims, whose truths they believed when inserting the word "Gospel" in their "Fundamental Orders", the first of our birthing documents and further written papers; this was the "True Religion" of the Founders. It was because of so auspicious and unique a beginning that life in America has had a distinct flavor, with comfort and promises on her way to greatness, and with an exceptionalism that, sadly, is about to disappear since our culture adopted a faulty theory about life - not the truth about its origin and thus, for the second time believing the Enemy of Life, and not the Creator of life.

For the world, and for America in particular, since she still has the power to lead, though now weaker for her faithlessness, the "Repentance unto life" must today include Repentance Unto God as Creator - a God purposely creating us, not patiently looking on for millions of years while human life, supposedly evolved by itself in swamps and caves; a "species" finally progressed on its own into sentient human beings now capable of absorbing the grandeur and beauty of a fathomless universe and even finding themselves now equipped and ready to explore it.

Who are we? We are beings of immense value which our Creator thought worth creating and redeeming.

"And a highway shall be there, and a way, and it shall be called, the way of holiness; the unclean shall not pass over it; but it shall be for those: the wayfaring men, though fools, shall not err therein."
(Prophet Isaiah).

SEVENTEEN

"TIS MYSTERY ALL"

*"... a Mystery is not something we can know nothing about: it
is only something that the mind cannot wholly know. It is to be
thought of not as a high wall that we can neither see over or get
around: it is to be thought of rather as a gallery into which we can
progress deeper and deeper, though we can never reach the end - yet
every step of our progress is immeasurably satisfying".*
(F. J. Sheed)

Whoever we are, when, convicted by the Holy Spirit of
our rebellion against a righteous God of Creation which
obscures the true meaning, worth and purpose of life, we turn
to our Incarnate Creator, we start to understand who we really
are in God's sight. This gift of understanding comes in the
wake of personal redemption. For sure, we can't immediately
learn the full import of what is scheduled for us in the world
just opened before our inner vision; but what we do know
at first sight is enough to overwhelm us, and to allow us to
properly understand the gift of salvation as the means for
the expected transformation of our life. The Judeo/Christian
Holy Scriptures is the best guide to sinners to the place where
redemption ceases to be just a doctrine and becomes a personal
experience. The truths in the sacredness of its pages plant in
us the seeds of repentance and faith. Then, light comes in the
glory of redemption, and you start seeing life as God sees life,
the meaning of it, the purpose of it, the eternal glory of it. This
new and revolutionary understanding of life came to me in a
flux of light, strangely enough, while simply hugging my wife,

though, as the slow learner that I am, not before I had read the Bible through many times.

The phenomenon of redemption personally experienced is something which I, and millions of individuals before me, have actually tasted. Afterwards, you'll be always wondering, as I do today, how you could have managed to live for years without the irreplaceable resources for living a life of growing fullness that God's redemptive work provides. I think of it as a pilot flying an airplane in the fog with the instruments that enable him to fly "blind" out of order.

This new understanding of life is bathed in joy, a joy of the kind which no circumstantial joys can match or sorrows extinguish; *"joy unspeakable and full of glory"*, as St. Peter, the transformed fisherman, strove to describe this feeling in his writings. It comes with the continuing realization of more and more of life's meaning and worth, while treading "The way of holiness" that Isaiah prophesied about - the way we discovered through the road sign that reads: "To the Incarnation and Redemption -'*The Way, the Truth, and the Life*' ".

"God is no man's debtor". This auspicious truth expressed in biblical words has given me the right measure of confidence in that fog I found myself in before the instruments I needed to travel safely. Our Creator, *"in Whom is life"*, is never reluctant to share His Own life with those He created to bear His image and likeness. Any living person today can be "Surprised by Joy" in the words of C. S. Lewis, the transformed intellectual and former agnostic.

The outcome of experiencing God' life in you is breathtaking. In discovering this truth about who you were reborn to become and is now commencing to be, light starts flooding corners of your mind where mysteries making you unsure about key issues of life were hiding. You find yourself no longer disturbed by doubts and fears which, though powerless now, still may besiege you. You no longer see your life as the perplexing thing it seemed to you before. You are able to realize that even despite the apparent unconcern with the evil and suffering which we might read in God's silence about unpleasant realities, He is, nonetheless, the apotheosis of love. You learn that limited human minds and fluttering hearts are utterly incapable of apprizing such love, for it is so beyond the best of what we can imagine as good. You start encountering this love everywhere, often surrounding you and enveloping all things. Like thousands before him, Charles Wesley, the creative 18th century composer of classic hymns, sings about his own transforming experience in words only poets and geniuses can put together:

"Tis mystery all! The Immortal dies! Who can
explore this strange design?
In vain the first-born seraph tries to sound the
depths of love divine!
'Tis mercy all! Let earth adore, let angel minds
inquire no more.
Long my imprisoned spirit lay fast bound in sin
and Nature's night;
Thine eyes diffused a quickening ray, I woke, the
dungeon flamed with light;
My chain fell off, my heart was free; I rose, went
forth and followed Thee.
Amazing love! How can it be that Thou, my God,
shouldst die for me?"

As I try my hand at sharing what I have been learning more each day about that mystery pregnant with joy, I ask the reader to see in your mind's eyes the cumbersome things in life that make living a burden, not a pleasure trip; to think of how the means which human culture come up with to ad meaningfulness to life while still in a state of rebellion against our Creator come short of filling our hearts full. I might have to go into a flight of fancy in trying to explain the inexplicable, but there is no other way but imagery to say what Godly wordsmiths tried to express about the wonders of Redemption.

Even the very articulate St. Paul acknowledged finding himself speechless when experiencing God's mysteries himself. So, here is my "take":

After undergoing this transforming experience, the first thing you discover, as I did, is that you are a different kind of being from the one you thought you are as learned from our present secularism. Though made to be more aware now of your bent for sinning, you find yourself drawn closer to the One who died to atone for your sins and to share His Own life with you. Even while having reason for discouragements because of the usual life tribulations, you notice growing points of light in the darkness of your personal unfavorable circumstances telling you of a haven of rest immediately ahead. You sense that these lights point to a permanent resting place at the end of your journey. Your mustard-size faith starts to grow along with your love for God as you read in your Bible that *"... all things work together for good to them that love God..."*.

When looking back on your life, the sting you feel for sins you have committed start to vanish at the sight of God's Grace as you learn from the Holy Scriptures that God remembers them *"no more"*. Besides this phenomenon which will certainly keep you from the psychiatrist's couch, you'll soon find out in God's Word that *"... I [God] will restore to you the years that the locust hath eaten"* and you soon learn exactly what that means to you.

You stop resenting not having attained yet your heralded "life potential", or the possibility that you might have already missed it because of your inability of meeting the often inflationary payment required. You know that the attainment of your true life potential comes already written in your soul's genetic blueprint, programmed to be reached at the appropriate time as it relates to eternity; and that until then, you can still pursue that potential right here and now, without the anxiety and fear of the damaging side-effects connected with its achievement in the limitedness of time and abilities. You know

now that its fullness will be unfailingly attained when you are to soon dwell permanently in the eternal unlimitedness of the realm you were created for.

You are assured, as you go along your earthly journey, that all this life-changing new knowledge coming from the experience you went through, despite its newness to you, is a natural and not so rare phenomenon. You are gratified to read and hear about other wayfarers who lived through the same experience and had their lives also transformed by it, even if in circumstances much different from yours. You know, even before finding this truth confirmed in your Bible, that your personal redemption has started to return you to the divine nobility of the original Creation. You find out that you are unlike anyone else not just because of your fingerprint or any other of the multiple marks of your individuality, but because you are one of a kind; because your role in the drama of a fathomless universe was written by the most knowledgeable and prolific of writers, especially for you, at the time of your conception.

You are now conscious that you are, indeed, not only worthy enough to have been conceived in the mind of a purpose-driven Creator - but you also find yourself increasingly yearning for that Godly purpose which keeps drawing you to what is Godly, even while you are becoming conscious of being more human, with all the human nature's weaknesses, limitations, and shortcomings - warts and all. You find being confirmed by your own experience what the Bible teaches - that on embracing personal redemption one becomes, in a manner of speaking, "the residence of two persons", what the Scriptures call the *"the old man"* and the *"New Man"* ; yet, you know that, definitely, you are not a victim of the whimsical "split personality" of Psychiatry's diagnosis. If you had heard but "didn't get it", now you understand the classic anecdote of the simple man telling someone that since his new birth into God's Kingdom it seemed that there are two dogs fighting within him (asked who usually wins, his answer, which is very biblical, was: "the one I feed the most"). You begin to understand why many physicists are convinced today that there are more than just three dimensions in things; that they could well be right, for you know now that you do have a cosmic connection with the reality of things eternal without your having been involved in Eastern mysticism. You discover that you are now equipped to live in the realms of both time and eternity, each with its distinct laws and values. You learn to identify which issues of life belong to each realm, how they relate to each other, and how to practically conciliate the two, this, resulting in a peace of mind you never experienced before.

You know now that there is a reason why you were born, that there is both an earthly and an eternal purpose for your life. Even the few glimpses of this purpose you are able to perceive give your life all the meaningfulness you need as a source of contentment, no matter what unpleasantness you are facing for a time or are called upon to keep on enduring. Because of this truth, you realize that to be a human being is to partake of an exquisite adventure, even while surrounded by evil, dangers, and suffering which are still integral part of earthly living. Expectations of coming pleasures suffuse your inner being with quiet joys which you recognize as forerunners of raptures to come. You start seeing evil, suffering, and even death, for what Redemption has made them to be - the shadows that beauty and truth need on this sinful earth to finalize the sketching of life as the final masterpiece. You realize with a breath of relief that the brushes of life's Enemy now being dipped in dark paint are soon to be forever destroyed, together with the paint itself - and that at any time, any time at all.

Your new understanding of yourself immediately begins to revolutionize your life in your relationship to God, things and people, and especially with your marriage partner if you have one. You realize that this new understanding is what elevates the value of human life beyond anything you can think of - a truth that applies of all of human life, whether within or outside the womb, whether youthful or nearing death, whether in the innocent toddler, or in the former willing sinner once imprisoned in the darkest cell of humanity's sinfulness, or within the rare individual who has reached a saintly status. You realize that this high worth of human life is universal and the same to all individuals, whether a person is wealthy or poor, cultured or illiterate, sick or healthy, ugly or beautiful, black or white, yellow or brown; that this makes human life to be the richest of gifts - to be prized when perceived for what it is; to be held securely, the fullness of its coming joy to be consummated in eternity, a promised fullness that lends meaning and hope to you throughout your earthly life, no matter what your circumstances may be. For what you have discovered fills your mind with everything that human reason can perceive as sources of wellbeing, bringing you into a state of inner peace you never thought possible. Because of this, you find yourself being a spontaneous doer of what is good, without having to be constrained or threatened in order to do it.

You can wake up every morning knowing for certain that whatever news you are to hear that day, or the events in it affecting you, your loved ones, or the whole human society, your inner joy will remain, even if the news and events are of a tragic nature and your heart is still assailed by fears, tears, and doubts. This is the human life our gracious Creator wants us to have - a life purchased by the Incarnate and suffering Redeemer with a price too high to be assessed by the powers of the limited human mind. A mystery indeed, to be fully unveiled amid the fullness of eternal joy at the gates of the Eternity we were created for.

Best of all, you'll find that human life as depicted here is not the fancy of wishful dreamers, positive thinkers, or idealistic mystics; that despite all the appearance of being too good to be true, human life is the actual love-inspired work of the Creator of Beauty Himself - the Beauty of Holiness - to be placed at the center of the picture of wonders of His cosmic creation. And you are assured that there was nothing wrong with your mind before and throughout the astonishing disclosure of who you really are now.

Lastly, in keeping with the message of this book, as a cradle-American or as an American By Choice, your real you is that citizen now ideally qualified to help re-establish and keep this nation's identity in her distinctiveness of people's self-governance and all other features that made America great; a people living under God, in a Nation established Under God, and in the end of time, absorbed into God's promise of a Kingdom of Heaven established forever on a New Earth and a New Heaven.

The alternative of not starting to partake of God's life through personal redemption even while on this earth is so tragic as to be beyond words. A gifted writer who experienced this life after spending most of his years as an unbeliever, succeeded better than most in articulating the only two diametrically opposed alternatives and their eternal consequences:

"...the dullest and most uninteresting person you can talk to may be one day a creature, which, if you saw it now, you would be strongly tempted to worship, or else a horror and a corruption such as you now meet, if at all, only in a nightmare...It is in the light of these overwhelming possibilities, it is with the awe and circumspection proper to them, that we should conduct all our dealings with one another, all friendships, all loves, all plays, all politics. There are no ordinary people. You have never talked to a mere mortal. Nations, cultures, arts, civilizations - these are mortal, and their life is to ours as the life of a gnat. But it is immortals whom we joke with, work with, marry, snub and exploit - immortal horrors or everlasting splendors."
(C. D. Lewis)

EIGHTEEN

FOR SUCH TIME AS THIS
THE CHALLENGES OF TWO
KINGDOMS

Many years ago, there was an orphan girl who lived in a prosperous nation. Her family had come from another Country. The young girl was raised by an uncle, and they became affluent with the goods of their hostess-nation. The damsel was a beautiful girl. She became the wife of the Emperor and lived in his palace. Soon after becoming Queen, she had to face an incredibly difficult, life-or-death decision. She learned that the vast Empire where she lived was about to be bathed in blood because of a religious-political upheaval that disturbed the nation. The alien youth knew what was about to happen, but under a law decreed by the Emperor, to tell him without being asked could cost the girl her own life. While she agonized over the decision whether to tell him what she knew, her wise uncle challenged her with these words: "[If you don't tell the Emperor]...*thy father's house shall* [also] *be destroyed: and who knoweth whether thou art come to the Kingdom* **for such time as this?**" Despite the danger she faced, the courageous girl confronted the Emperor with what she knew, and because of her bravery, countless human lives were spared, including her own and that of her uncle.

If you are familiar with the Judeo/Christian Scriptures - and you need to be if you are to understand what is happening in the world today - you would know that this story is not a fairy tale. It is a chapter of history that tells of an event that happened centuries before Christ. The girl's name was Esther. Her uncle's name was Mordecai. To this day, once a year, now for over two thousand years, the Jewish people celebrate Esther's life and heroism. They call this celebration the Feast of Purim.

By reading the Bible you would know why, unlike other races, the Israelites never saw their nation lose her identity to the world, though it was for a long time dissolved in the geopolitical pages of history; why, though geographically dispersed, they dwelt for thousands of years in all the nations of the world without losing their Jewishness. You would understand why historians unanimously teach that Western Civilization with all its cultural and scientific accomplishments is rooted in the contents of the Judeo/Christian Scriptures and the culture they inspired; that America was their latest, and possibly, their last feat. You would understand also that that is why the America of the New World and the newly recovered Israel have today the same deadly enemy; why both nations share the cross-hairs of a common enemy's weapons of death. You'll finally learn, as I did, that as people who fear the Judeo/ Christian God of America's Founders, your life and mine are connected with the uniqueness of both nations - America and Israel - for the Incarnate God of Creation, to save the world, was born a Jew. And, finally, you'll learn why I am convinced today that, like Esther and Mordecai, as immigrants also, we could be here "for such time as this", for knowing what most Americans don't know, either for having never been taught, or for having been made to ignore.

You and I have much in common with Mordecai and Esther. We, too, live now in this unique Country, the most affluent nation that has ever existed in World History. We have been gladly partaking of her blessings and generosity. We know that this Nation has been freer and wealthier than other nations because at her beginning her Founders did all the right things to create the proper habitat for humans to live and thrive in; that this ideal atmosphere for human living was formed by spiritual values and a polity derived from the Judeo/Christian Holy Scriptures. For two centuries her leaders and mentors succeeded in maintaining those truths culturally and politically, and America prospered beyond their dreams.

But today, even while we enjoy this Nation's prosperity, she is in the midst of a life-and-death struggle. And we know what most Americans seem not to know.

Being truly the "land of the free", from her birth there have always been ideological struggles in her society. Since the last Century, contention between two opposing worldviews has developed into a full-fledged cultural war. One party wants to keep her as conceived and reared, "under God", thus securing her success as a nation. The other party, turning its back on the Judeo-Christian God of her Founders and on His Biblical principles which guided her conception and growth, has been fighting to change her into a Nation to be like all other Western nations now steeped in a secular humanistic worldview. A new generation of political leaders and academicians is utterly rejecting the Judeo/Christian worldview which has distinguished America as an exceptional nation.

The culture war has turned out to be a War for America's Identity between "progressives", those who want this nation's identity to be "changed", and conservatives who know that, divested of her true identity, America will not only cease to be the unique nation she has become, but will cease to be altogether. And today, those who want a vanishing America are winning. The casualties of this war already surpass the number of soldiers who died in all our foreign wars while defending this Country, the dead so far being mostly would-be Americans killed in the womb. Fifty millions of them have already died since abortions were legalized in 1973. At this writing, every 26 seconds another little American is killed in this Country, often under horrendous, barbaric procedures. The chances of those who believe in America's true identity being not thoroughly defeated have become critically smaller since the last general election. The consequences of conservatives not immediately starting to win major battles is unthinkable - the inhuman killings will increase in number, with the old, the ill and the "unfits" added to that number; and we will continue to lose our freedom, our well-being, our good living standard,and the ability to defend ourselves against America's avowed enemies, both those outside our borders and those living among us. Incredible as it sounds, America's leaders and academia are turning against both Jews and Christians.

Those of us who came to live in this Country primarily for what America is - her values, her humaneness, her God-fearing, nuclear-family orientation - and not only for what she can give materially, cannot fail to heed what our conscience and reasoning, stirred by gratitude to a Nation that has given us so much, are now telling us:

[If you don't join heart and soul with those who are fighting for the true America whose identity expresses itself in God, faith, family, and individual freedom] "*... thy father's house shall* [also] *be destroyed: and who knoweth whether thou art come to the Kingdom* **for such a time as this?**"

Like Esther, Mordecai, and the Pilgrims, the "*First Comers*" to America - we immigrants were born elsewhere. If, like me, you are like Esther and Mordecai, you know something that could save a multitude of lives, including, possibly, the lives of your own children, and, someday, the lives of your elderly parents and unhealthy family members whose sentences of death are already being sought. The spiritual seed of the Judeo/ Christian Scriptures which fathered America is the same which inseminated your soul with a love for God and family. Our spiritual birth and the birth of America came out of the same womb fashioned by the same Incarnate God, the Redeemer of humanity. America is our sister. Because of this, you and I can recognize the mortal danger America faces today. We are able to see it better than most politicians and often better than cradle Americans unaware of what is truly happening. We know what can keep this nation as the America that attracted us to her soil. We know that America is a child of faith in a God of Creation, the only faith that gives human life its true worth for being created in the Creator's own image and likeness; a faith that provides not a platform for death, but for life, *"and life more abundant"* - something that once made America the safest Country for people to live, establish themselves, and raise a family.

Migrations have been, historically, a powerful force behind cultural changes. The Archenemy of life has often cunningly used migration as a weapon for the decimation of human life. We can see his hand behind contemporary events when we read statements like this from an imam speaking for Al Qaeda: *"One of the goals of immigration is the revival of the duty of jihad and enforcement of their power over the infidels. Immigration and jihad go together"*. These words give one of the many reasons why the Judeo/Christian worldview on which Western Civilization was built has been under heavy attack for many years, especially since Darwin and the increase of secularism. Today, that worldview is being practically dismissed from European thinking and is about to be totally rejected by America. This ennobling view, with the high worth it attributes to human life, found its best practical expression on the shores of America in the 18th Century, but now it is vanishing here too. Because it was used as the basic foundation of America, she saw immigration become a contributing force for her growth, freedom, and a better life, not for further wants and early deaths. It was only because of the Judeo/Christian worldview bonded to her identity that she was able to build on immigration her affluence, her security, and her greatness. Are we to let her down now?

Europe is already under siege by the forces of secular humanism inimical to Jews and Christians, and America, the last rampart able until now to keep the archenemy of life at bay, is being demolished by her own children. We, late-coming Pilgrims and immigrants, could well be the ones who have come here **for such time as this** to possibly become the decisive force in preserving the America which that God-honoring worldview created. The enemies of America have already won many great battles, but the Cultural War itself is still being fought. As most of us know, the Pilgrims' God is not dead, as some claim. The Pilgrims' America can still survive if you and I, as 21st Century Pilgrims, join the battles **with the weapon we have, prayers on our knees, and ballots in our hands with the right votes**.

If we ignore or minimize the danger this Nation is facing today we are either in denial, or we are too enraptured by the prosperity and the on-going materialism in which we participate, to pay much attention. Too many of us are already seeing our children and grandchildren being lost in the Godless environment of the present secularized culture. It is possible that all that most of us know of what is really happening here and in the rest of the world is through the 15 to 30 minutes of daily slanted information articulated by an anti-God, anti-family, anti-America, and anti-Israel media. Some of us have known how government-controlled media in our country of birth was used as an instrument to bring tyranny about. As God-fearing immigrants to this Nation, we have an obligation before the God of her Founders to take the time to fully realize the serious state America is in today. We must become thoroughly acquainted with the issues of this tragic War of Identity already filling America the Beautiful with corpses of babies, despairing, suicidal teenagers, and other war casualties from sea to shining sea. Then, being aware and challenged, we must seek to learn what action God expects from us, individually and as a group. I suspect that we shall have to answer before God's Court someday for having been brought here at this crucial stage of America's history "for such time as this", and having not done what was required of us. It is very possible that America's life and the lives of our children's depend heavily, if not solely, on whether we respond to these challenging words echoing through the centuries and now filling our ears - *"who knoweth whether thou art come to the Kingdom for such a time as this?"*

As we predispose ourselves to heed the challenge to help save America's soul, it is crucial for the life of our own souls to understand that when creating us, our Creator had eternity in mind. And the Bible teaches that, unlike His creatures, He never changes His mind. As a place for our earthly sojourn, America is but a waiting-room He has graciously made comfortable and pleasant for cradle-Americans and Americans By Choice to be in while waiting for His promise of a New Heaven and a New Earth. Through the Judeo/Christian Holy Scriptures, we can learn that it is possible that God could today be getting ready to call those who acknowledge and love Him to enter through the door and into that world and then close forever the curtains of the cozy waiting-room called America.

For many years I allowed myself to love this Nation above the place "prepared for those who love God". Though at first sight praiseworthy, that was wrong. For years, like the secularists I blame for America's maladies, I looked at earthly life as having a meaning of its own; that the picture of life could be made clear and pleasant enough without that point outside the frame, the "Point of Infinite" of my mother-tongue. I discovered how wrong I was when I learned that the Creator-God honors the understanding of life which has showered America with samples of earthly blessings as illustrative samples of eternal ones; that the truth about life has eternity for its kernel; that earthly life, both of individuals and nations, with its shortcomings, suffering and sin-issued death-sentence is a temporary stage of preparation for a coming Kingdom of Righteousness and joy.

Today, I think of America as our Creator's practical presentation to humanity about the glory of God's Kingdom, her blessings being the items of "show-and-tell". Because of this, I pray for our Nation more than ever, that she might yet have many years left as the America her God-fearing Fathers founded. For there are two other Kingdoms competing today with God's Kingdom of Righteousness: there is the secular-humanists' *"Kingdom of Mammon"*, as the Bible calls the Kingdom of Man which internationalists are trying hard today to put together politically, and there is the sensuous Kingdom or Islam being planned to be established in the world with weapons and killings. Both of them offer no preparatory Redemption, no "beauty of holiness" in their landscape. Though the Judeo/Christian Scriptures assure us that God's Kingdom will eventually prevail, an America as conceived by the Pilgrims will go a long way to cut down the number of victims to be made by the other two in their attempt to succeed. But that is a subject for another book, though readers can learn all about it by carefully studying their Bibles.

A true spiritual renaissance is the only event that can save America now from the present danger she faces, as this will bring back true orthodox conservatism. Politics and Parties alone will no longer do. Historically, spiritual revivals have repeatedly saved America from the demise which has befallen other nations. It **can** happen again. I believe that praying earnestly in our various languages for the gracious Nation that has adopted us as her children can be the answer to America today. I have no doubt about the Pilgrims' God being still open to having the torch of spiritual revival once more lit in America's growing darkness.

We have all the right reasons to believe that America doesn't have much time left to live as the Country that so powerfully attracted us to her shores for having been all these years a Nation Under the God of Creation. But we must live today as if the end is not yet in sight. God loves us too much not to keep that pleasant waiting-room open for us a little longer, though now we know that that is for the purpose of seeing "the light of life" and for more souls to gain admission into the real Promised Land. Until then, because of what is taking place in our world today, that which we must do must be done quickly and in earnest. We must act as if God's grace could expire at any moment if not met by gratitude at the heart's door of God-fearing, family-loving foreigners living in America today. America is hurting today, and so is the God she was conceived by and lived under for so many years. We must seriously consider whether, unknown to us, we have been brought here at this crucial stage of America's history "for such time as this". Could it be that America's life and the lives of our children depend heavily, and, perhaps, crucially, on whether we respond to those challenging words echoing through the centuries and reaching us in this Twenty First Century in which lives created by the God Who is love are so terribly threatened?

May every American By Choice's heart respond to the challenge before the present growing darkness covers forever "The City on a Hill".

EPILOGUE

"AMMI" OR "LO-AMMI"?
(THE CHOICE IS OURS)

"Then said God, Call his name Lo-ammi: for ye are not my people, and I will not be your God... Say unto your brethren, Ammi...it shall come to pass, that in the place where it was said to them, Ye are not my people, there it shall be said to them, Ye are the sons of the Living God." (The Prophet Hosea)

"I have set before you life and death, blessing and cursing; therefore choose life, that both thou and thy seed may live." (Moses)

We were presenting a musical program in another nursing home to a new group of Alzheimer's patients. This time it was a little lady who was getting all the attention. The audience was already settled, listening enthralled as Olivia played her harp. All, except Judy. The little, wiry lady was still going through her usual routine of which we were previously warned. Somehow, what she was doing seemed very important to her for a reason known only to her: she kept walking toward each person in the room, one at a time, her face earnest and tense. She would get close and look intently at each person's face for a while before moving to the next one. We were told beforehand that she was always doing this to people wherever she was. Whom or what she was looking for nobody knew. She never said anything, for she no longer spoke. She had not talked since dementia invaded her mind and had, somehow, silenced her.

Judy was still moving from person to person, quietly, persistently, when Olivia, now at the piano, played the introduction to the song we had chosen for me to sing. By this time Judy had her back toward me as she moved from person to person, still closely inspecting every face. Consciously directing to Judy the message contained in the words, I made sure my heart joined my voice in singing:

> Great is Thy faithfulness, O God, my Father.
> There is no shadow of turning with Thee;
> Thou changest not, Thy compassions they fail not;
> As Thou hast been Thou forever wilt be.

As I started singing that first stanza, Judy abruptly stopped where she was and quickly turned her full attention to me. All eyes were on her now, the people anxious to see what she was about to do. Judy walked, briskly, to where I stood and halted right in front of me. Even while I sang, she was looking me in the face, closely, silently, studiously, the way she had been doing for a long time to everyone she met. But now an extraordinary thing was happening: Judy's face was breaking into a happy, loving smile not seen on her before. Suddenly, she found her voice. In a crisp, beautiful alto she joined me in singing, as naturally as if she had never stopped being a normal person, her now rejuvenated face still close to mine:

> Great is Thy faithfulness! Great is Thy faithfulness!
> Morning by morning new mercies I see;
> All I have needed Thy hand hath provided.
> Great is Thy faithfulness, Lord, unto me!

As we experienced together the unexpected miracle, there was no doubt in my mind: Judy had found what she had long been looking so long for, something which her weakened mind must still have been able to connect with a human face, producing a familiar melody with a meaning vital to her, a meaning which the ravages of Alzheimer's decease could not destroy. With my voice now cracking, I had to force myself to keep on singing with Judy. The people in the room, their eyes also brimming with tears, listened, enraptured, as the song of hope continued, now with Judy and I singing in duet:

Summer and winter, and springtime and harvest,
Sun, moon and stars in their courses above
Join with all nature in manifold witness
To Thy great faithfulness, mercy and love.

Pardon for sin and a peace that endureth,
Thy Own dear presence to cheer and to guide;
Strength for today and bright hope for tomorrow,
Blessings all mine, with ten thousand beside!

Judy knew all the verses by heart. Her clarity of mind lasted long enough for her to join the group at the end of our program in singing "God Be with You Till We Meet Again". Long enough to assure me that what comes from God cannot be totally forgotten by a weakened or manipulated mind of people or of Nation; that the everlasting truths are still there, etched on the soul of both by God Himself, with His own fingers, as He did with the Ten Commandments on tablets of stone - still there, whole, ready to be restored to memory in time and eternally translated into a disease-free world; that a nation which has been purposely, wisely conceived and reared under God could still be made to remember who she is, in the same way she was made to forget.

Judy, taken by dementia, remembered. America, deceived, can still be made to remember having in her youth opened her arms to a Creator God, and having been once honored by Him with goodness and greatness before an admiring world. And having remembered, may she once again rise in Godliness, once again may she be an example to the world of what glory our Lord can bestow upon a nation that truly lives "Under God", steadfastly trusting in Him until He returns in all His glory on The Last Day.

IN OUR CONVOLUTED 21ST CENTURY, UNLESS, LIKE
THOSE WHO CONCEIVED OUR NATION, WE START
THINKING ABOUT OURSELVES AS ETERNAL SOULS
LIVING IN TEMPORARY BODIES, NOT AS BODIES WITH
(OR WITHOUT) SOULS, AMERICA SHALL CONTINUE
TO DECLINE INTO EXTINCTION AND TAKE WESTERN
CIVILIZATION ALONG WITH HER.

APPENDIX

A PROMISE AND A PRAYER OF HOPE FOR AMERICA, ISRAEL'S YOUNGER SISTER

"IF MY PEOPLE, WHICH ARE CALLED BY MY NAME, SHALL HUMBLE THEMSELVES AND PRAY, AND SEEK MY FACE, AND TURN FROM THEIR WICKED WAYS, THAN I WILL HEAR FROM HEAVEN, AND WILL FORGIVE THEIR SIN, AND WILL HEAL THEIR LAND."

"O LORD, THOUGH OUR INIQUITIES TESTIFY AGAINST US, DO THOU IT FOR THY NAMES' SAKE: FOR OUR BACKSLIDINGS ARE MANY; WE HAVE SINNED AGAINST THEE. O THE HOPE OF ISRAEL, THE SAVIOUR THEREOF IN TIME OF TROUBLE. WHY SHOULDST THOU BE AS A STRANGER IN THE LAND, AND AS A WAYFARING MAN THAT TURNETH ASIDE TO TARRY FOR A NIGHT? WHY SHOULDST THOU BE AS A MAN ASTONIED, AS A MIGHTY MAN THAT CANNOT SAVE? YET THOU, O LORD, ART IN THE MIDST OF US, AND WE ARE CALLED BY THY NAME; LEAVE US NOT."
(II Chron. 7:14 and Jeremiah 14:7-9).

About the Author

DECIO DE CARVALHO came to America in his twenties for further studies, after graduating from college and International Flight Control. It was as a foreign student in America that he finally understood the true meaning of the word "Gospel" as understood and lived out by the Pilgrims. While living here he discovered that this understanding finally provided him the answers to what he calls "The Puzzle of America" in her uniqueness as a nation and "The Puzzle Of Life" in its diversity, yet simplicity. Decio has also published "The Other America", written as a novel and designed to warn parents of school-age children how that our children were being conditioned in their schooling to accept the kind of America now being hastily formed by secularists and deists.

After a few years with a missionary movement where he helped plan and launch the first ocean-going ship for education and evangelization, the de Carvalho's developed a music ministry for senior citizens, especially Alzheimer's patients. The globe trotting couple, married now for over 50 years, "hang their hats" in the little burg of Lake Ariel, Northeast Pennsylvania.

CPSIA information can be obtained at www.ICGtesting.com
Printed in the USA
LVOW032037231011

251714LV00001B/1/P